Green Smoothies

50+ Recipes for Nutrition, Life, and Health

By Nadia Joyner

First Printing, 2012

Printed in the United States of America

Table of Contents

Introduction

I have absolutely fallen in love with Green Smoothies and I want the world to know it! Every day, Green Smoothies have changed and continue to change the lives of all my family members and so many others around the planet. In fact, I've honestly lost count (a long time ago!) of how many people have thanked me for sharing what I know about Green Smoothies. I appreciate their gratitude, but I tell them that I am only spreading the news about the wonderful gifts that nature provides for us. I'm simply a humble messenger. I only know that I am fully committed to drinking Green Smoothies every day for the rest of my life – and I'm going to continue to get as many other people hooked on them as I can!

Throughout my 20+ years as a personal trainer and fitness coach, the concept of optimal nutrition keeps coming up. My students always have questions and with each new class, the same questions get asked over and over again. I'm happy to answer because that's my job! What it's taught me is that most people just need a little information and motivation to begin to understand just how important proper nutrition is for all of us and how living a healthier lifestyle can be fun and exciting! Worldwide, humans are engaged in never-ending personal battles to get in shape and increase longevity – and countless millions who simply don't understand or have never been exposed to proper dietary guidelines. People may sincerely desire to be healthy and remain as youthful as possible, but they just don't understand how.

That's just where Green Smoothies come into the picture!

To put it clearly: Green Smoothies are nutritional superstars that can change your body and your life from the inside out. It's amazing how powerful it is to introduce and maintain proper nutritional balance into your life! Like all living organisms, the human body is a predictable biological machine that can be manipulated into states of superior health. However, in order to accomplish this, an individual must make sure of at least a couple of things.

Proper Foods and Daily Exercise!

It's no secret to most that exercise and nutritious diet choices are the two main factors of health that we humans can control. It's our choice to be physically active or not on a daily basis and it's also up to each of us to choose the right foods and beverages to deliver the nutrients we need to thrive. If we choose not to engage in physical activity or if we choose to ingest unhealthy food sources, then we are left to live less healthy lives than we could. Pretty simple really, right?

Hint: Green Smoothies make healthy food intake delicious, ultra-simple, and rewarding!

In most cases, people assume that getting and staying in control of their bodies is an incredibly complex matter better left for the determination of physicians, biologists, and other types of scientific leaders, but that's not true! In fact, developing and maintaining increased health and fitness is a relatively straightforward matter.

Here are the two main focus points you need to accept:

1. You have to move your body by exercising on a daily basis.

2. You have to take in the nutrients that your body requires to function efficiently.

If you can accept the truth of these two guidelines, then you are already well on your way to achieving the health goals that have long eluded you.

It's really that easy!

For many people, exercise is a dreaded act. Even though physical activity can be extremely enjoyable, there are those who just can't stand the thought of it! They may claim to really want to become more physically active, but they continually put off initiating an exercise plan. Likewise, many people erroneously believe that ensuring proper nutrition is an endeavor that will be unpleasant, distasteful, and difficult.

In my family, exercise is an accepted and expected element of our daily routines. It adds meaning, health, and enjoyment to all of our lives and we would live less contentedly without it. It's the same now with Green Smoothies: everyone in the family loves their daily, tasty, and ultra-healthy Green Smoothies! Just drinking one each day becomes an enjoyable habit that you can be proud of. You'll live a healthier, energy-filled, and natural lifestyle that will benefit everyone you have relationships with. Trust me! Best of all, it will benefit you the most!

A Brief History of Human Food Intake

Millions of years ago before industrialization, globalization, computerization, and urbanization, human beings were in much closer contact with the earth. There were no fast food joints to frequent, no organized governmental bodies dictating our food choices, and no political and/or economic motivations forcing people to live and eat in certain ways. In fact, there was just the need to survive. Food choices were quite limited according to an individual's location, climate conditions, and their abilities to successfully hunt and gather.

Obesity was seldom an issue for our prehistoric ancestors. Starvation was by far a larger concern. In general, the human diet consisted of natural plant products that could be gathered. Occasionally, when a hunt went well, the animal products that were consumed were low in fat and without chemical additives like steroids, antibiotics, pesticides, herbicides, and other harmful substances. Everything was eaten fresh because there were no preservatives. Preservation methods had not been invented yet.

Approximately ten thousand years ago, agricultural practices surfaced across the planet, providing ready sources of grains, milk, potatoes, and other dietary staples. Additionally, the diversity of available meats and vegetables greatly increased. However, with this increased availability came issues of contamination, infestation, and more. People had to develop ways of protecting, storing, and preserving their food sources. Cooking became main-stream and food preservation became a major societal concern.

As time passed, the world became more aware of the importance of food. Scientific minds questioned the ways in which food really affected us. Somewhere along the way, people started to understand the important relationship between our health and the foods we ate.

Fast Food History Facts!

* 400BC is when Hippocrates (the "Father of Modern Medicine") proclaimed: Let food be your medicine and medicine be your food!

* In the 16th century, Leonardo da Vinci compared human metabolism to a burning candle (a very accurate analogy!).

* In 1747, Dr. James Lind discovered that lime juice could spare British sailors from scurvy. Although the discovery was totally ignored for four decades to follow, British sailors eventually became known as "Limeys."

* During 1770, Antoine Lavoisier uncovered the fact that body heat is a result of food oxidation during digestion and assimilation.

* Carbon, nitrogen, oxygen, and hydrogen were recognized as the four main constituents of the foods we ate in the early part of the 19th century.

* In 1847, Justus Liebig reported that sugars make up carbohydrates, fatty acids were comprised of fats, and amino acid chains create proteins.

* In the 1860s, Claude Bernard proved that fat could be manufactured from proteins and carbohydrates. This meant that blood glucose energy is able to be stored as either glycogen or fat.

* In the early 1900s, Carl Von Voit and Max Rubner both earned independent credit for first measuring the expenditure of energy in living organisms.

* In 1911, Casimir Funk combined the words "vital" & "amine" to form the word "vitamin."

* A year after that, Elmer McCollum discovered the first fat-soluble Vitamin: A. He also discovered the first water-soluble vitamin: B. (Of course, by 1915, Vitamin B "grew into" the Vitamin B complex, comprised of several different water-soluble vitamins.) Additionally, he finally gave a name to that mysterious substance that is known worldwide now for preventing scurvy: Vitamin C. (This guy liked to keep his naming simple!)

* During the 1930s, William Cumming Rose instructed us on essential amino acids, the building blocks of all-important protein.

* 1941 was the first year that a RDA (Recommended Daily Allowance) chart was established for vitamins.

* After the Industrial Revolution, various methods for storing and preserving food sources were created. These include milling, pressing, drying, cooling, heating, irradiating, and more. While these methods can be useful at cutting down on food-borne pathogens, they also partially deplete the nutritional values contained in foods.

* During the 1960s, families became less in touch with nature and became centered mainly in urban conglomerations. Two-income families became prevalent. People spent less time cooking and preparing healthy meals at home because of their busy life schedules. Fast food joints sprang up like weeds in the jungle – and obesity/disease rates began to skyrocket!

Since then, you probably already know the rest of the story. Preventable diseases are at all-time high rates. Many studies state that more than a third of Americans are classified as "Obese."

Americans are putting themselves in very serious danger because of the foods they choose!

It makes me so sad every time we travel to the city and see all the people walking down the crowded sidewalks. So many people are obviously suffering, physically and emotionally because they're carrying far too much weight. They develop unhealthy eating habits and continue to make poor food intake decisions – and after years and years passing by, they find themselves experiencing various health problems, not knowing quite what to do about it.

When I see all those people on the sidewalks, the looks of fatigue on their faces as they simply attempt to walk, I think of some of my long-time friends and about how they are literally falling apart physically. That's one of the biggest reasons I find it so easy to stay motivated about the Green Smoothie lifestyle: every day, I see how Green Smoothies positively affect all of the different sorts of people that I know!

Even if everything else seems to be going wrong, we can all still blast our systems with raw, organic nutrients every day in the form of Green Smoothies and still come away feeling good. We're sharper. We have more energy. Our bodies are fortified with huge amounts of free radical destroying antioxidants and plenty of other nutrients. We're generally healthier from head to toe and that is a good thing no matter how you look at it!

Still, more than 1 in 3 Americans are now overweight and/or obese.

Current Stats on American Health

* Average weight of US woman: Over 165 pounds.

* Average weight of US man: Over 195 pounds.

* Obesity is strongly correlated with almost every health concern, including various cancers, cardiovascular issues, diabetes, stroke, high blood pressure (hypertension), arthritis, and so many more.

* In 2009, health care costs in the US were approximately $2.47 trillion dollars. By 2019, that price tag is expected to rise up to about $4.5 trillion.

* Health care insurance rates have risen 300% faster than wages over the past 10 years.

* In 2009 alone, the top five health insurance companies in the US reported more than $12.2 billion in profits.

* In 2008, there were more than two dozen big pharmaceutical companies that made over 1 billion dollars in profit (each) from sales within the US.

* Nearly 50% of all Americans are on some type of regularly prescribed prescription medication.

* The majority of Americans are classified as "completely inactive" by health professionals from all fields.

Leading Causes of Death in the US

It's so sad when someone we know and love dies, but people do pass on and in so many cases, far too soon. It really makes me upset that so many people who die do so prematurely for no reason at all, except they just didn't remain committed to their own levels of health while they lived. Many smoke tobacco products, drink heavily, never exercise, eat high fat, high-sodium foods, and generally live like they want to die. What really gets to me is that many people seem oblivious to the fact that the majority of deaths by disease are completely preventable.

Even after someone is diagnosed with a specific disease or health condition, like colon cancer for example, they can still reverse the symptoms of the disease. In many cases, they can dissolve the malignancies completely by making positive lifestyle modifications that increase their health. According to the most recently published statistics from the Center for Disease Control (CDC), the leading causes of death in the US by percentages are:

* Heart disease: 24.5%

* Cancer: 23.3%

* Chronic lower respiratory diseases: 5.6%

* Stroke (cerebrovascular diseases): 5.3%

* Accidents (unintentional injuries): 4.8%

* Alzheimer's disease: 3.2%

* Diabetes: 2.8%

* Influenza and Pneumonia: 2.2%

Note that heart disease and cancer kill almost 50% of the total population! Guess what health professionals worldwide cannot deny?

What we eat has an incredible ability to prevent, stop, treat, and/or reverse the onset and development of almost every health condition imaginable!

The point that I'm making is that in order to thrive and live long, you have to incorporate an organized approach to nutrition into your life. There's no way around it. The great news for all of us is that Green Smoothies deliver a stunning amount of unspoiled, miraculous nutrition in every mouth-watering, health-loaded serving! I'll be blunt and just say that drinking Green Smoothies regularly will add years to your life and make you far more able to enjoy the years you have while you're alive.

Those are just a few more reasons why I am so committed to the Green Smoothie lifestyle. Green Smoothies make everything better for everyone!

Remember this:

1. Exercise is very enjoyable!

2. Healthy food intake with Green Smoothies is delicious, simple, and fun!

In order to understand how Green Smoothies can become a daily force of complete positivity in your life, we should probably first understand a little more about the history of the human diet. We need to see where we came from (in a dietary sense), where we are, and why. Don't worry - this will be short and sweet!

Free Radicals and Antioxidants

I promise not to bore you to tears with too much scientific talk throughout this book, but there are some key concepts that need to be addressed so that we all can truly appreciate why and how Green Smoothies are so good for us! It really is amazing to consider the nutrient value of a Green Smoothies, especially when you compare it with the nutrient values of so many other commonly consumed food sources.

Anyway, one of those key concepts involves free radicals and antioxidants. Somehow we all seem to know the two are related, but how? Why are free radicals bad for us and how do antioxidants help to prevent and/or reverse the damage they cause?

I always knew I needed to understand how free radicals and antioxidants have so much meaning to human health. One day, I just dove in and studied up on the subject! I'm glad I took the time because now I understand how much control I have over my own health. Put simply, antioxidants help with the power to block free radical damage from occurring - and even to neutralize the free radicals altogether! Let's take a closer look:

Free Radicals

Simply defined, free radicals (or just radicals) are unstable, organic molecules. It's widely accepted now that free radicals have a lot to do with cellular damage, the onset of certain diseases – and even aging! Saying that radicals are unstable refers to the fact that they are missing an electron from their atomic structures. They know they're unstable too!

In fact, free radicals travel throughout the body searching for easy molecules to bond with, steal an electron from, and then leave the previously healthy structure in an unstable form. They roam around freely and are able to steal electrons from a wide variety of other structures.

Free radicals are thieves and body wreckers that care only about themselves!

To be fair, radicals do have a couple of positive functions. First, they help phagocytes (white blood cells) consume harmful bacteria and pathogens that live inside the body. In addition, it is believed that free radicals play a key role in the redox signaling process, which transfers cellular messages.

When a free radical steals an electron from a cell wall, that structure is left unstable. It in turn becomes a free radical itself and thus creates a snowball effect of harmful damage throughout the body. Aging may not be altogether preventable, but much of the damage commonly caused by free radicals is. By reducing the number of free radical molecules present in your body at any given time, you are reducing your probability of experiencing an array of different possible types of cellular damage.

This accumulative damage is what adds up to aging!

Free radicals are largely created from environmental pollutants including smoke, herbicides, poisons, and other toxic substances. They are formed as a natural byproduct of human metabolism. Radicals are all around us most of the time. In the middle of America, it's quite difficult to escape regular exposure to free radical substances. The best key we humans have for reducing our exposure to them and thereby reducing our respective probabilities for experiencing their harmful effects is to blast these radicals with antioxidants!

Antioxidants

Antioxidants are organic molecules found primarily in vegetables and fruits that combat the numerous negative effects of free radicals. They are more specifically found in the vitamins that our food sources contain, especially Vitamins E, C, A (in beta-carotene form), and selenium. Additionally, antioxidants are found in high doses in natural plant chemical substances, aka phytochemicals.

Antioxidants are like powerful barriers that stop free radicals from causing cellular damage!

Just stick with me a little longer and we'll be through with this technical stuff. Then we can get on to the exciting, mouth-watering part of the book: Green Smoothies!

The Oxidation Process

Oxidation is a process which involves two basic occurrences:

1. Oxygen is added to a substance.

2. Electrons are lost from the substance.

Now, when electrons are lost as a result of oxidation, ionic molecules are created and called free radicals. As we know, free radicals are very detrimental to the body. In general, adding oxygen to a substance begins to break that substance down like an apple's meat turning brown as a result of contact with the air.

Like the apple, the human body breaks down as a result of exposure to free radicals, which are natural byproducts of oxidation.

More free radicals are created every time a person talks, eats, moves, exercises, or even breathes! All of these functions, anything and everything we do, produce more free radicals for our systems to face. That's why it's so important to have a very regular delivery schedule when it comes to fresh supplies of antioxidants.

By increasing the antioxidant content in the foods you consume, you will help your body to:

* Enhance immune system effectiveness.

* Reduce the chances of developing cardiovascular disease, various forms of cancer, and more.

* Slow down the aging process.

By increasing your intake of antioxidants, you significantly improve your body's ability to ward off disease and avoid all the other damages that free radicals can cause. As you might expect, fresh foods provide more ready, quality antioxidants than do supplements and other sources. Although antioxidants are available in many food sources, they are especially concentrated in vegetables (especially green, leafy varieties), fruits, nuts, legumes, whole grains, sprouts, and seeds.

It's not surprising that antioxidants are highly concentrated in lip-smacking, ultra-healthful Green Smoothies. By incorporating select antioxidant-rich ingredients in your smoothie recipes, you can stay loaded with them – and thereby, continually thwart the attempts of free radicals to cause any damages to your precious cellular structures!

Green Smoothies deliver loads of life-saving antioxidants, vitamins, fiber, water, minerals, and phytonutrients!

Why Green Smoothies?

In my career as a fitness coach and nutrition counselor, I've had such a blast helping other people meet and exceed their various health goals – and I've seen a lot of trends, diets, and other "health miracles" come and go like the wind. In most cases, health is maximized when we keep things natural.

Okay, so we understand that the importance of nutrition is undeniable. The simple matter is that in order to live a healthy lifestyle, fight off disease, and increase longevity, we have to embrace the guidelines of ensuring proper and hopefully optimal food intake decisions. Of course, this book is all about the sheer power and effect of Green Smoothies! Why Green Smoothies anyway? It's because they pack such a nutritional punch that they can't be ignored! Green Smoothies are the Mike Tyson of food power! They are lions in the food jungle!

8 Fast Green Smoothie Facts

1. Green Smoothies are absolutely loaded with vitamins and other very beneficial constituents, including minerals, antioxidants, anti-inflammatories, phytonutrients, bioflavonoids, fiber, water, and more!

2. Green Smoothies are stuffed with chlorophyll and chlorophyll is proven to be just one atom different in molecular structure than human blood. Drinking and assimilating the ready goodness of a Green Smoothie is much like receiving a cleansing blood transfusion!

3. When combined in the recommended 60% organic fruit and 40% green leafy vegetable ratio, Green Smoothies are very easy to digest. Follow the proper preparation guidelines (provided later) and blend your smoothies well. Adequate blending homogenizes the nutrients and makes them super-simple to assimilate. In fact, these delicious smoothies are so bio-available that they start to absorb into your system even while still in your mouth!

4. Although fresh-made juices are delicious and nutritious, they are not considered a real food source. That's because they have little or no fiber. Green Smoothies are considered a whole food source because they retain 100% of their natural fiber content.

5. Green Smoothies are totally delicious! Blended with about three to five fresh, organic fruits, Green Smoothies are dominantly sweet, but balanced with earthy, wholesome green leafy vegetable goodness. Children, adults, and even our favorite domesticated pets can benefit greatly from Green Smoothies. (My dog, Buckethead, is very fond of all Green Smoothie recipes. He slurps them up like he's gone mad!)

6. It's simple to make Green Smoothies – and clean up is a breeze too! I keep my fruits and greens in separate containers in the fridge. I have them ready to go so that it's always a streamlined process (more on this later). When I'm done blending the smoothie, I just rinse the blender jar and it's ready for the dishwasher. While the blender is running, I put the different fruit and green containers back in the fridge and I'm almost finished cleaning up even before the smoothie is made!

7. Any human being that's at least six months old can enjoy the natural strength of Green Smoothies. Babies love the sweet tastes. Toddlers think of

them as treats, teenagers love them, men and women alike appreciate the health benefits they pack, as well as the increased vitality they bring into our lives.

8. There are an unlimited number of Green Smoothie possibilities with which to experiment. That means that Green Smoothies are infinitely versatile. There's always another fruit/vegetable/green combination to experiment with. Everyone can have a favorite Green Smoothie recipe of their own!

Of course, I could go on and on about numerous other Green Smoothie benefits, but we will discover loads of these as we progress through this book. In the next sections, we will get into all of the super-healthy constituents of Green Smoothies. When you learn about all the unspoiled, nutrient-loaded goodness contained in Green Smoothies, you'll completely understand why they are considered by nutritionists and other health professionals worldwide to be the ultimate food source.

Let's learn about what makes Green Smoothies so awesomely healthy for us!

Nutrition of the Green Smoothie

The fact is that many people, billions in fact, make poor food choices on a daily basis. Now, I don't want to sound heartless. I understand that a large percentage of the world population has little to no choice concerning what they are privileged enough to eat. I'm talking about the rest of the population, those who do have choices about the foods they eat. So many people go through their lives giving no consideration to the enormous amounts of non-nutritious, even toxic, food sources that they take into their bodies.

Remember this: Anything you put into your body has to be broken down, extracted from, assimilated and/or disposed of by your body.

Fresh, organic Green Smoothies have very little to no harmful ingredients. In fact, they are some of the healthiest, most easily assimilated foods ever prepared. A closer look at just what's included in a Green Smoothie is definitely warranted. Let's check it out!

Water

It should be no major news flash that water is vitally important to life and health. Second in importance to maintaining life only to the air we breathe, water sustains us, heals us, and enables us to remain vital. Depending on which part of the body you consider, the human body is made up of between 22% and 90% water. For instance, your brain consists of about 90% water. Muscle tissue is made up of roughly 75% water and bone material is just about 22% water. Blood is more than 80% pure water. Overall, the human body is roughly two-thirds water.

Green Smoothies are also water-rich, just like our bodies! When you intake Green Smoothies on a daily basis, you increase the hydration in your life – and that's definitely a good thing! Dehydration causes a long list of health issues and water combats all of them in a powerful style. Taking in more water will help your body to:

* Efficiently transport oxygen and nutrients throughout your body

* Think clearly

* Keep the air you breathe moist to keep your lungs functioning well

* Enhance metabolic functioning

* Shield vital organs from harmful substances and organisms

* Regulate its temperature effectively and efficiently

* Keep the liver and blood detoxified

* Keep its joints lubricated

* Plus more

It's true that every cell from the bottom of your feet to the top of your head needs water. Without adequate and regular hydration, things get ugly fast on a cellular level. So, keep blending up those ultra-tasty, water-rich Green Smoothies to keep your cells hydrated and thriving!

Fiber

Fiber is a substance made up of non-digestible plant threads and/or filaments. Although your body cannot digest fiber, it is nonetheless very important for developing and sustaining optimal health. It has been repetitively proven in clinical studies that diets high in fiber are extra helpful at:

* Maintaining a healthy digestive system

* Controlling blood-glucose levels

* Lowering cholesterol

* Preventing the development of cancerous cells

* Maintaining a healthy weight

Making sure you take in plenty of fiber is an important step toward developing optimal health and it just so happens that Green Smoothies are naturally loaded with life-enhancing fiber. Yes! Yet another fact about Green Smoothies that make them an undeniably intelligent food choice.

Vitamins

There's always a lot of talk about vitamins. I remember my dad going on a Vitamin kick back in the early 1970s. He gave me niacin (Vitamin B3, nicotinic acid) and I must have been deficient in it because it made me feel really warm. From then on, I had a fascination with vitamins, although it took me many years afterward to really take the time to properly learn about vitamins. Everyone seems to have an opinion and that's fine, but as it happens, there are a lot of misconceptions about vitamins too.

Just what are vitamins and what roles do they play in developing and sustaining human health?

Vitamins are scientifically defined pretty simply. They are just organic compounds essential for metabolism. To date, thirteen vitamins have been identified. Vitamin-like substances known as bioflavonoids (see phytonutrients) are strongly believed to bring about a vast array of beneficial health advantages. If an organism is deficient in one or more vitamins, it may develop specific disorders, as determined by which vitamin or vitamins is/are deficient. So, it's a good thing that it takes just a tiny bit of vitamins, normally just a milligram or two of each daily to remain in good health.

There are fat-soluble and water-soluble vitamins. Fat-soluble vitamins include A, D, E, and K, while the B complex Vitamins (Biotin, Folate, Niacin, Pantothenic Acid, Riboflavin, Thiamine, Vitamin B6, Vitamin B12), and Vitamin C comprise the water-soluble list. Our bodies are capable of storing fat-soluble vitamins in our liver, but water-soluble vitamins are not well stored. For this reason, we need to keep resupplying ourselves with water-soluble vitamins on a regular basis.

Here are just a few things that our body uses vitamins for:

* Healthy, glowing skin, and hair

* Strong bones, teeth, and nails

* Blood clotting ability

* Night vision

* Maintaining muscle tone

* Manufacturing blood cells

* Metabolizing energy

* Normalizing blood-glucose levels

* Synthesizing antibodies

* Healing wounds

* The list goes on and on!

Green leafy vegetables and other delicious, colorful vegetables are the best sources for life-yielding vitamins. Green Smoothies are one of the world's absolute best sources for delivery of unspoiled, raw, organic vitamins, all types of them! Every Green Smoothie you drink is loaded down with all-important vitamins. Your body and brain will be thanking you and thanking you!

Minerals

Minerals are made up of inorganic matter vital to human health and survival. They are neither plants nor animals. It's interesting that minerals are what are left over in the form of as, when materials from plants and/or animals are burned. Our human bodies are roughly 4% minerals.

There are macro, micro or "trace," and electrolyte classifications for minerals. The macro-minerals are so named because they are needed and stored in larger quantities than most other minerals. The macro-minerals include calcium, magnesium, and phosphorous. Micro or trace minerals are more numerous and include:

* Chromium

* Copper

* Fluoride

* Iodine

* Iron

* Manganese

* Molybdenum

* Selenium

* Zinc

Then, there are the three electrolyte minerals: sodium, potassium, and chloride. These three minerals are special because they actually conduct electrical charges within the body to help accommodate muscle contraction and nerve function. They also keep the body's fluid levels balanced.

We need minerals to perform a variety of functions including:

* Manufacturing hemoglobin

* Developing and maintaining strong bones and teeth

* Protecting cells from oxidative damages

* Synthesizing metabolic enzymes

* Manufacturing digestive juices

When you incorporate daily Green Smoothies into your life, you enter into a zone of internal power that's difficult to beat down. You guessed it – Green Smoothies are also one of this planet's best sources for vitality-enhancing dietary minerals!

Phytochemicals (Phytonutrients)

Phyto is Greek for "plant" and so phytochemicals refer to the natural chemical compounds found in plants. Scientists speculate that there may be as many as 10,000 phytochemicals, many not yet discovered that may be very beneficial for the prevention, treatment, and/or reversal of various human health issues, including cancer, metabolic syndrome, stroke, cardiovascular disease, and many more.

The phytochemical nutrients found in Green Smoothies are amazing antioxidants that have the power to annihilate free radicals. There are many different types, including zeaxanthin, kaempferol, tannins, carotene-alpha & beta, lutein, and many others. Each has its own strengths, but none have any weaknesses.

By diversifying your Green Smoothie ingredients, you maximize your intake of a variety of life-enhancing phytonutrients!

Thousands of years ago, people figured out that certain elements in certain food sources were very effective at treating their health conditions. If you go back less than 200 years, plant-based medicines were all people had. There were no big pharmaceutical corporations back then. There were no AMA-certified medical doctors pushing the big pharmaceutical products. There were only traditional healers who used medicinal plants to help people feel better, treat disease, and maintain health. It wasn't that long ago!

Different phytonutrients provide different health benefits. That's why it's important to diversify your choices between Green Smoothie ingredients. Mix it up folks! When you do, you will be rewarded with a nice medley of fibrous materials, antioxidants, anti-inflammatories, and much more. Just remember that cooking and other forms of manipulating fruits and vegetables diminish the content of nutrients in them. So, consume yours in whole form.

Although there are various choices available between phytochemical extracts and supplements, it's always best to gain your organic phytochemical nutrients from whole food sources. The raw fruits and green leafy veges in Green Smoothies provide loads of many different phytonutrients. Of course, munching all those fruits and vegetables constantly takes a lot of time and makes the jaws quite sore. What can be done you ask?

The answer is deliciously obvious: gain daily supplies of wholesome, raw-form phytochemical nutrients by drinking Green Smoothies!

Greens, Fruits, and Vegetables

One of the things I love most about Green Smoothies is that you never have to drink the same type twice (unless you want to). There are an infinite number of recipes that you can easily create, depending on the types of nutrients you want to include in them. You can blend up an Orange-Strawberry-Baby Spinach Green Smoothie to blast your cells with antioxidant power or even a Cranberry-Asparagus-Kale Green Smoothie to help detoxify your body and blood.

Whatever the case and whatever a person's particular needs, Green Smoothies are an intelligent, economical, and very effective approach to developing and maintaining optimal health levels. Consider the following greens and fruits, as well as hundreds of others readily available whenever you're set to enjoy your next fortifying Green Smoothie!

Before we get into the Green Smoothie recipes, we need to go through some more nutrition education. It's what makes Green Smoothies the amazing food sources they are! After all, this is a book to learn valuable information from – AND have a lot of fun! So, let's get the science out of the way so we can get into blending up some super-powerful, life-saving Green Smoothies.

6 Popular Types of Green Leafy Vegetables with Nutritional Information

Green leafy vegetables are some of the best food sources available to humans. For thousands of years, people have benefitted from their high levels of vitamins, minerals, antioxidants, anti-inflammatories, detoxification agents, carotenoids, flavonoids, and more. That's why Green Smoothies are so incredibly powerful as dietary constituents. When you regularly ingest green leafy vegetables, you give your body what it needs to resist the attacks of oxidation, inflammation, toxification, and much more!

Cabbage

Cabbages along with Brussels sprouts, broccoli, and cauliflower, are a member of the cruciferous vegetable family. Although the different types of cabbages are not as nutritious overall as some other family members, they are still loaded with vital nutrients that will make your Green Smoothies healthy, energizing, and naturally tasty!

Cabbage is an excellent source of Vitamin C, a natural antioxidant. It's very low in calories and contains an impressive amount of fiber. Red cabbages have roughly twice the Vitamin C of green cabbages. On the other side of the coin, green cabbages contain roughly twice the folate as do red cabbages. Cabbage is helpful at preventing colon cancer and other malignancies associated with estrogen stimulation.

1 cup of raw green cabbage has:

* 20 calories

* 33 mg of Vitamin C (54% RDA)

* 85% RDA Vitamin K

* Provides a good source of magnesium, calcium, iron, thiamine, phosphorous, potassium, Vitamin B6, and manganese

* Almost no cholesterol

* Almost no fat

* Almost no sodium

Chard (Swiss Chard)

Swiss Chard or just chard is a green leafy vegetable that displays red stalks, leaf veins and stems. It's known for its sweet beet-like taste and delicate texture. Scientists have discovered that chard has thirteen unique polyphenol antioxidants including kaempferol, syringic acid, and betalains.

I love using Swiss Chard in my Green Smoothies, maybe even more than I like spinach!

The phytonutrients in chard, among other functions, help it to live up to its worldwide reputation as a champion antioxidant, blood-glucose stabilizer, anti-inflammatory, and detoxifying agent. In short, Swiss Chard is one of the world's best food sources. It's a nutritional powerhouse vegetable that you should definitely enjoy on a regular basis!

In addition, just 1 cup of raw Swiss Chard contains:

* 715.9% DV of Vitamin K

* 214.3% DV of Vitamin A

* 52.5% DV of Vitamin C

* 37.6% DV of magnesium

* About 30 calories

* A good source of potassium, iron, fiber, copper, calcium, protein, choline, zinc, and more.

Collards

Becoming a larger star in the raw food arena, collard greens are packed full of vitamins, minerals, phytonutrients, and deliciousness like few other foods have been, are, or will ever be. Collards are nutritionally similar to kale, but are a heartier, chewier green leafy vegetable. Its taste is on the stronger side than kale. The leaves of collard greens are wide and large.

Collard greens are a superior agent for binding to bile acids throughout the digestive tract. That means that collards are an excellent digestive enhancer, but that's certainly not all! That strong bile acid- binding ability makes collards very effective at lowering cholesterol (which bile acids are synthesized from).

Collard greens are amazingly powerful - and scrumptious!

Additionally, collard greens are gaining a huge reputation as a cancer inhibitor. That's because of their unique combination of four separate glucosinolates: gluconasturtiian, glucotropaeolin, glucoraphanin, and sinigrin. All four can be converted to ITC (isothiocyanates), which kick in detoxification and anti-inflammatory systems, helping to thwart the development of cancer.

1 cup of raw collard greens provides:

*   1045% DV of Vitamin K

*   308.3% DV of Vitamin A

*   57.6% DV of Vitamin C

*   More than 40% DV of manganese and folate

*   A good source of Omega-3 fatty acids, iron, potassium, phosphorous, Vitamin B6, choline, tryptophan, and more

*   50 calories

* Antioxidant properties

* Anti-inflammatory properties

* Support for cardiovascular health

* Support for efficient digestion

* Lowered cholesterol

Kale

Loaded up with Vitamins K, A, C, and more, Kale is notorious for lowering the risks associated with developing prostate, ovary, breast, colon, and bladder cancer – and probably many other types as well! Like collard greens, kale has a nice assortment of ITCs (isothiocyanates) that help the body fight cancer.

Kale is highly concentrated with two very powerful types of antioxidants: flavonoids and carotenoids. There are at least 45 different flavonoids in kale, increasing its value as an effective anti-inflammatory agent.

Kale makes you feel strong and good looking!

Kale is now recognized as providing comprehensive support for the body's detoxification system. New research has shown that the ITCs made from kale's glucosinolates can help regulate bodily detoxification at a genetic level. Its ruffled leaf edges range in color from black to purple to cream and more, all dependent on the variety of kale you select. Kale has an earthy taste that is not overpowering.

Every 1 cup serving of raw kale provides:

* Defense against cancer

* Cardiovascular support

* Lots of fiber

* 1327.6% DV of Vitamin K

* 354.1% DV of Vitamin A

* 88.8% DV of Vitamin C

* A good amount of copper, tryptophan, Vitamin B6, potassium, Omega-3 fatty acids, iron, magnesium, and more

* Just 35 calories

Spinach

Perhaps the most beloved green leafy vegetable of all, spinach is one of the planet's super foods for a lot of excellent reasons. To begin with, the vibrantly green leaves of spinach appeal to the eyes and nourish the body in uncountable ways. Spinach is certainly my personal favorite green leafy vegetable! Its dark green color is created by plenty of carotenoids, including lutein and zeaxanthin, which are known to reduce macular degeneration.

You'll see that I talk A LOT about spinach. I love it!

Additionally, more than a dozen flavonoids are present in spinach, making it an excellent anti-inflammatory and anti-cancer agent. Spinach is a stand-alone champion amongst green leafy vegetables in that it is the only one that contains a special group of flavonoids called methylenedioxyflavonol glucuronides. These little nutrients of power have been shown to demonstratively slow down the cell division in human stomach cancer growths.

Calorie for calorie, spinach is famous for being the world's most nutritious food – out of all of them! That's a powerful distinction – and the primary reason why I choose spinach for the majority of my personal Green Smoothie recipes. Mild tasting and unbeatable in nutritional content, spinach is an amazing food source that can lengthen and better your life!

1 cup of raw spinach provides:

* 1110.6% DV of Vitamin K

* 377.3% DV of Vitamin A

* 84% DV of manganese

* 64.7% DV of folate

* Loads of Vitamin C, Vitamin B2, calcium, potassium, iron, fiber, protein, zinc, and so much more

* Anti-inflammatory and anti-cancer benefits

* Cardiovascular benefits

* Almost zero fat and cholesterol

* Very low sodium

* Glycemic load of zero

* Less than 10 calories

Turnip Greens

Tasty, stuffed, and filled with all types of beneficial nutrients, turnip greens are difficult to beat as a complete food source. Their slightly bitter taste is a result of their incredible calcium content. Although turnip greens are effective at providing numerous health benefits, they stand out amongst other green leafy vegetables in their ability to fight the development of cancerous cells. This is because turnip greens affect three separate bodily systems simultaneously:

1. The detoxification system

2. The anti-inflammatory system

3. The anti-oxidizing system

Especially helpful at preventing cancer development, turnip greens are also strong supporters of cardiovascular health, digestive efficiency, inflammation reduction. and more. These mean greens have been cultivated for thousands of years by people all over the planet. Turnip greens are super-nutritious, extra delicious, and are an ultra-healthy plant food that will make your Green Smoothies taste robust and deliver optimal vitality!

1 cup of raw turnip greens provides:

* 661.6% DV of Vitamin K

* 219.6% DV of Vitamin A

* 65.7% DV of Vitamin C

* 42.4% DV of folate

* Plenty of manganese, calcium, fiber, copper, Vitamin E, Vitamin B6, potassium, iron, and much more

* Less than 20 calories

* Glycemic load of 1

* No fat, no cholesterol, and very little sodium

So there you have it, six wonderfully healthy green leafy vegetables to include in roughly 40% of every Green Smoothie you blend up! Of course, there are many others too. Consider experimenting with broccoli greens, mustard greens, bok choy, arugula, quinoa, and more. Green leafy vegetables are nearly impossible to beat as overall nutritional food sources and mixing them with fresh organic fruits to make Green Smoothies is a no-brainer for taste, fun, and ultimate health!

Various Types of Fruits & Vegetables with Nutritional Information

Now it's time to consider some of the nearly unlimited choices you have when it comes to the fruits and vegetables available to mix into your Green Smoothies. The roughly 60% of fruits and vegetables you use will add deliciousness, texture, and even more vital nutrition to your recipes. Below are just some of my personal favorites, but there are so many others.

Experiment. Use your imagination. Let your taste buds and sense of adventure guide you. There are no wrong choices!

Acai

Everywhere you look nowadays, there is a buzz about acai berries. The fruit from the Central/South American palm is known scientifically as Euterpe oleracea. The berries from the acai palm are about an inch long and are red/purple in color. That deep coloring is the result of a high content of a specific type of phytonutrient called anthocyanins. Foods with high levels of anthocyanins like blueberries, strawberries, and acai berries are powerful antioxidants, helping those that ingest them to deny the development of cancer, heart disease, and more.

I am crazy about acai berries!

Acai berries also contain various flavonoids. Food sources with all these antioxidants are known to help protect cellular structures in general. They neutralize free radicals and help the body remain free of inflammation and toxicity. In fact, healthful foods like acai berries are so powerful that they actually help slow down the aging process, leading to increased longevity and life enjoyment.

Each 100g serving of acai berries will add the following to your delicious Green Smoothie recipes:

* Anthocyanins, including cyanidin-3-galactoside, ferulic acid, delphinidin, resveratrol, and petunidin

* Pro-anthocyanidin tannins like protocatechuic acid, epicatechin, and ellagic acid

* More than 200 healthy calories

* Anti-proliferative properties that inhibit carcinogens from binding to DNA molecules

* Oleic acid and linoleic acid (Omega-9 and Omega-6 fatty acids) that help lower LDL (bad) cholesterol levels, raise HDL (good) cholesterol levels, and prevent heart disease

* Good source of dietary fiber

* Lots of potassium, manganese, iron, copper, niacin, riboflavin, and Vitamin K

Asparagus

One of my family's favorite vegetables to add into Green Smoothies is asparagus (Asparagus officinalis). Members of the Lily family, asparagus is heavy on potassium and contains natural phytochemicals that help the body to detoxify. Because of high respiration rates, asparagus needs to be consumed quickly after harvesting in order to maximize nutrient content.

Asparagus also contains special nutrients called saponins known for their anti-inflammatory and anti-cancer strengths. Specifically, asparagus contains asparanin A, protodioscin, sarsasapogenin, and even small amounts of the widely researched diosgenin. Put simply, asparagus can help to keep your blood pressure and your blood-glucose levels stable.

1 cup of raw asparagus provides:

* 13.4 mg of Omega-3 fatty acids

* 53.6 mg of Omega-6 fatty acids

* 70% DV of Vitamin K

* 20% DV of Vitamin A

* 32.3 mg of phytosterols

Avocado

The fruit from avocado trees (Persea americana) is distinct from the majority of other fruits in that they are high in mono-unsaturated fat content and therefore, calories. That's the same type of fats found in olive oil, and very heart healthy. Their nutritional content is comparable to many nuts and seeds. Avocados have a soft, buttery, subtle flavor that can be added into various Green Smoothie recipes without changing their primary taste.

Avocados have more soluble fiber than any other fruits. They're also loaded with beta-sitosterol, a plant sterol that inhibits the absorption of cholesterol through the linings of the intestines. They also have more protein than any other fruit, at roughly two grams per four ounce serving.

Every 1 cup of avocado also provides:

* 28% RDA of pantothenic acid

* 20% RDA of folate

* 20% RDA pyridoxine

* Useful amounts of copper, Vitamin K, potassium, Vitamin A, and more.

Bananas

Bananas are low in fats, but relatively high in calories. That's because they contain a lot of sugars, including sucrose and fructose. They also contain very healthy amounts of vitamins, minerals, and antioxidating phytonutrients. The easily digestible meat of banana fruit quickly revitalizes the body, and is a top pick of athletes and other health-minded people everywhere.

I have never met one single person who didn't at least like bananas!

Bananas contain impressive amounts of polyphenolic antioxidant flavonoids, including lutein, beta-carotene, alpha-carotene, and zeaxanthin, all of which help you to protect your cells from oxidized free radicals and ROS (reactive oxygen species), widely believed to speed up the aging process.

For every 100 gram serving of banana, you get:

* 41% DV of pyridoxine (Vitamin B6)

* 23% DV of dietary fiber

* 33% DV of Vitamin C

* 23% DV of potassium

* Healthy amounts of magnesium, manganese, copper, and Omega-3 fatty acids.

Beets

In order to understand the value of a beet, you need to understand a bit about toxic metabolites called homocysteines. Homocysteines are defined as amino acids that occur as intermediates during the metabolism of methionine. These damaging metabolites are heavily correlated with the development of CHD (coronary heart disease), peripheral vascular disease, and stroke.

Beets are a strong source of a particular phytonutrient compound called (glycine) betaine. It's the compound that gives beets their naturally dark red color. Betaine lowers the levels of homocysteines found in the blood. Green Smoothies that contain healthy amounts of delicious, sweet beets possess curative powers that are difficult to match.

Beets are the sweetest vegetable known. Beet juice is used to sweeten various fruit juices!

The greens of beet roots are also storehouses of nutrients that include Vitamin A, flavonoids, and carotenoids. These nutrients are good for keeping your vision in shape, for healthy skin, and also help prevent the development of cancerous cells. So when you're preparing your beet roots for your Green Smoothies, just go ahead and throw the tops right into the mix as well. Beets come from the same plant family as Swiss chard (Amaranthaceae-Chenopodiaceae) and are loaded with natural goodness that your body needs!

In addition, with every 1 cup serving of raw beet roots, you give your body:

* Only about 45 calories

* Very little fat, cholesterol or sodium

* 15.2% DV of fiber

* 37% DV of folate

* 22.5% DV of manganese

* Healthy amounts of Vitamin C, potassium, Vitamin B6, and more.

Blueberries

One of the few fruits indigenous to North America, blueberries are succulently sweet and absolutely loaded with life-enhancing antioxidants! In fact, there are very few fruits, regardless of where they're from that have higher antioxidant contents than blueberries. In the US, blueberries rank second in berry consumption only to strawberries.

The ORAC (oxygen radical absorbance capacity) rating of blueberries is an amazing 5562 TE (Trolox equivalents). The active antioxidant compounds in blueberries are classified as polyphenolic anthocyanidin compounds and include tannins, quercetin, myricetin, chlorogenic acid, and the ever-demanded kaempferol. Then, when you add in their natural supplies of flavonoid antioxidants like zeaxanthin, carotene β, and lutien, you have a holistic concoction of health that makes cancer cells shriek in terror!

All things considered, blueberries offer the following benefits for your health:

* Good source of fiber

* Loads of antioxidants

* Healthy amounts of Vitamin C and iron

* Lower blood sugar and control blood-glucose levels

* Protect against cancers, infections, general aging, degenerative diseases and cardiovascular disease.

Additionally, with every cup of raw blueberries, your body receives:

* 35.7% DV of Vitamin K

* 14.2% DV of fiber

* About 75 calories

* Healthy amounts of iron, copper, manganese, zinc, and potassium

* Good amounts of B-complex Vitamins including pyridoxine, pantothenic acid, folate, niacin, and riboflavin.

Cherries

Cherries are sexy, exotic, and sophisticated as fruits go. One of the lowest calorie fruits, cherries are a powerful way to amp up the nutrient value of your Green Smoothie recipes. They are juicy, tasty, and compliment just about any flavor combination. Like blueberries and pomegranates, cherries are loaded with pigment. Pigment is where all those madly healthy polyphenolic flavonoid compounds and strong antioxidants.

Specifically, cherries contain solid amounts of carotene-beta and zeaxanthin. Cherries are loved worldwide for their ability to help fight off aging, cancer, neurological disease, and diabetes mellitus. Note that there are more than one thousand varieties of cherries worldwide.

My teenage son once ate an entire 1-pound bag of cherries in under 30 minutes!

Because cherries are rich with anthocyanins, they act as anti-inflammatory agents that reduce the onset and development of health conditions, including gout, fibromyalgia, arthritis, and others. Cherries also contain melatonin, another antioxidant known for battling headaches, neurosis, and even insomnia. Additionally, cherries contain pectin, like apples, a substance proven to help lower LDL (bad) cholesterol levels.

And if all that weren't enough to send you out looking for organic cherry sources, cherries also are well-stocked with potassium, iron, copper, zinc, manganese, and other minerals.

Every 1 cup serving of raw cherries also gives you:

* 35% DV of Vitamin A

* 20% DV of Vitamin C

* Almost zero fat, cholesterol, and sodium.

Garlic

Onions, leaks, and garlic are all members of the Lily family, also known as the Allium family. Few food sources ever discovered have earned the fame and love that the reputation of garlic offers and that's largely due to the fact that garlic is a healer. The healing properties in garlic stem from three important compounds, all of which contain sulfur. Those three are:

1. Thiosulfinates (best known for allicin)

2. Sulfoxides (best known for alliin)

3. Dithiins (best known for ajoene)

These three types of compounds are responsible for the pungent odor presented by garlic – and they're also responsible for many of garlic's healthy benefits. Garlic contains plenty of other nutritional constituents including minerals, vitamins, and phytochemicals.

Delicious garlic is one of the world's most healing, mysterious plants!

Garlic, taken raw has the power to help the human body in many ways, including but not limited to:

* Inhibiting cholesterol production

* Reducing blood pressure

* Decreasing the development rate of coronary artery disease

* Lessening the chances for peripheral vascular diseases

* Preventing strokes

* Preventing stomach cancer

Garlic has strong anti-inflammatory, anti-bacterial, anti-fungal, and anti-virus properties. The bulbs of the garlic plant are some of nature's best sources of zinc, selenium, manganese, calcium, iron, potassium, and much more. Garlic also contains several immune-enhancing antioxidants, including carotene-beta, zeaxanthin, and good ole' Vitamin C.

A 100-gram serving of raw garlic healthily provides:

* 95% DV of Vitamin B-6 (pyridoxine)

* 52% DV of Vitamin C

* 26% DV of selenium

* 33% DV of copper

* 18% DV of calcium

* 21% DV of iron

* 73% DV of manganese

Grapes

First cultivated by Egyptians over seven thousand years ago, grapes are one of nature's miracle foods. They possess loads of minerals, vitamins, and all-important polyphenolic antioxidants found in their skins and seeds. While red and purple grapes contain an abundance of anthocyanins, white and green varieties are famous for their tannins, specifically catechin. Grape cultivars from the United States are known scientifically as Vitis labrusca and Vitis rotundifolia, while their European relatives are known as Vitis vinifera.

Grapes are perhaps known best around the world for their resveratrol content. Resveratrol is a powerful antioxidant that has been shown to provide protection against colon cancer, prostate cancer, CHD (coronary heart disease), Alzheimer's disease, various degenerative nerve diseases, and more. Additionally, grapes are appreciated for their ability to naturally regulate blood-glucose levels, prevent viral/fungal infections, thwart inflammation, and treat allergic reactions.

Oh yeah, they make good wine too!

1 cup of raw grapes will provide your body with:

* 33% DV of manganese

* 16.8% DV of Vitamin K

* Healthy amounts of Vitamins C, B6, and B1

* 172 mg of potassium

* Very little fat or cholesterol

Kiwi

Also known as Chinese gooseberry, kiwi fruit is scientifically named Actinidia chinensis and belongs to the Actinidiaceae plant family. It is the national Chinese fruit, native to the Shaanxi Province. Kiwis are classified as semi-tropical and deciduous.

Besides being high in fiber, kiwis are gifted with high Vitamin C content. They also contain healthy amounts of Vitamins A, K, and E, as well as other antioxidants, Omega-3 fatty acids, and minerals, including potassium, iron, and magnesium.

The list of kiwi's health benefits is long and includes:

* Protection from colon and other types of cancer

* Cardiovascular fortification

* Preventing neurological issues, including Alzheimer's

* Lessens the risk of stroke

* Hinders the development of ADHD, autism, and various other developmental issues

* Helps to naturally regulate blood-glucose levels

* Strengthens bones

With every 75 gram raw kiwi fruit serving you get:

* Only 60 calories

* 3 grams of fiber

* 154% DV of Vitamin C

* 34% DV of Vitamin K

* 312 mg of potassium

* 14% DV of copper

* 34 mg of calcium

Lemon

Lemons (Citrus limon) come from the plant family Rutaceae. Juicy and tart, lemon is one of the most demanded citrus fruits on the planet, trusted by the masses for its many health advantages. Thought to have first been discovered in the foothills of the Himalayas, lemons contain loads of Vitamin C and a special bioflavonoid compound called rutin. Also found in buckwheat, apples, lime flowers, and eucalyptus, rutin has been shown to:

* Strengthen blood vessels

* Protect against hemorrhagic strokes

* Treat hemorrhoids

* Prevent mucositis (a hurtful side effect of many mainstream cancer treatments)

* Treat osteoarthritis

* Reduce risk for CAD (coronary artery disease)

* Protect against some cancers

The tartness of lemons is due to their high content of citric acid. Citric acid helps dissolve kidney stones and assist with digestive processes. Lemons have no fat, no cholesterol. and are high in fiber content. Lemons contain impressive amounts of the flavonoid glycosides hesperetin and naringenin, free radical scavengers that reduce inflammation and boost immune system power. Lemons have an ORAC rating of 1225 TE (Trolox equivalents) per 100 mg.

Every 100 gram serving of lemon fruit also gives your body:

* Healthy amounts of B-complex Vitamins pyridoxine, pantothenic acid, and folate

* Copper, iron, calcium and potassium

* 88% DV of Vitamin C

* Bioflavonoids carotene-alpha, carotene-beta, lutein-zeaxanthin, and crypto-xanthin-beta

Mango

Known amongst scientists as Mangifera Indica, mango fruits are unique, mouth-watering, and packed with nutrients like few other fruits. Like cashew and pistachio nuts, mango fruits come from the plant family Anacardiaceae. Hailing from India, mango trees are seasonal and tropical. The juicy, sweet flavor from the orange-yellow mango is just slightly on the tart side.

Mango fruits are very helpful to human health for a variety of solid reasons. Mangos are proven to be effective at:

* Protecting against colon, breast, prostate, lung, oral cavity, and bone cancers

* Maintaining healthy skin and mucous membranes

* Controlling heart rate and blood pressure

* Protecting against infections

* Lessening risk of stroke

* Helping to efficiently manufacture red blood cells

When you mix mangos in your Green Smoothies, consider using them peel and all. The peels are also loaded with life enhancing phytonutrients and really do nothing to disrupt the taste or texture of your smoothies.

With every 100 gram serving of mango, you also get:

* 70 calories

* 46% DV of Vitamin C

* 156 mg of potassium

* Only 2 mg of sodium and .27 grams of fat

* 12% DV of copper

* Carotene alpha and carotene beta, as well as lutein-zeaxanthin

Peaches

Peaches (Prunus persica) originally come from China originally. Ripe, juicy peaches are loved worldwide, not just because they are so uniquely delicious, but also because they offer us an impressive array of health benefits. You see, peaches have a full tank of minerals, vitamins, and those life-saving antioxidants we all love: phytonutrients!

Peaches have no saturated fats and provide just 39 calories per 100 gram serving. They serve as powerful antioxidants, showing off an ORAC (oxygen radical absorbance capacity) value of 1814 Trolox equivalents (TE) for the same sized serving. Antioxidants in peaches include Vitamin C, lutein-zeaxanthin, cryptoxanthin-beta, and carotene-beta. These help to keep your body from being damaged from free radical attacks.

In addition, every 100 gram serving of raw peach fruit offers you:

* 1.5 grams of fiber

* 11% DV of Vitamin A and Vitamin C

* Healthy doses of B-complex Vitamins, including riboflavin, niacin, thiamine, and pantothenic acid

* 190 mg of potassium

* 0% sodium

* 7.5% DV of copper

Pomegranate

From Northern India, the pomegranate (Punica granatum) comes from the Lythraceae family of plants. Pomegranates are unique in taste, appearance, and most importantly, they're loaded with nutritional content! Along with mangos and some berries, pomegranates are known as "Super Fruits" because they are so concentrated with phytonutrient antioxidants, especially flavonoids.

Pomegranates have high levels of fiber too, four grams per 100-gram serving, making them effective for achieving healthy digestion, lessening the chance of stomach, bowel cancers, and a lot more. Pomegranates are an intelligent choice for those trying to maintain healthy weight levels and for those who wish to lower their LDL (bad) cholesterol levels. Pomegranates contain no saturated fats and each 100-gram serving supplies just 85 calories.

One of those most noted phytochemical compounds in pomegranates is called punicalagin, a powerful antioxidant that scavenges free radicals like a bloodhound goes after a fox! Along with tannins, punicalagin is very effective at hindering the development of heart disease and stroke. Pomegranate consumption on a regular basis has additionally been shown to thwart the advancement of diabetes mellitus, lymphoma, prostate cancer, and more.

Every lip-smacking serving of pomegranate fruit (4-inch diameter) also gives your body:

* 48% DV of Vitamin C

* 58% DV of Vitamin K

* 27% DV of folate

* 13% DV of thiamine

* 11% DV of Vitamin B6 and pantothenic acid

* 22% DV of copper

* 19% DV of potassium

Raspberries

Raspberries (Rubus idaeus) are from the Rosaceae plant family. They are native to Europe and have become one of the planet's most demanded foods. Why? Because they're packed with plentiful flavor, health, and versatility! Raspberries are also loaded with minerals, vitamins, and phytonutrients that are known to promote optimal human health.

It's interesting to know that raspberries are comprised of many "drupelets," arranged meticulously in a pattern, circling around and around a central, empty cavity. It takes between 80 and 100 drupelets to make up a single raspberry. Every separate drupelet is its own pulp container, enveloping a singular, very small, yellow-white seed. Each conically-shaped raspberry weighs between three and four grams.

Raspberries are concentrated with phytochemical flavonoid compounds including tannins, salicylic acid, gallic acid, cyanidins, catechins, quercetin, ellagic acid, anthocyanins, pelargonidins, and kaempferol. Together, these phytonutrients are known to combat the onset and development of many health conditions, including various cancers, heart disease, degenerative diseases, and aging in general. Raspberries are my personal favorite berry too!

Plus, each 1-cup serving of ultra-tasty raw raspberries you consume offers you:

* 54% DV of Vitamin C

* 32% DV of dietary fiber

* 41% DV of manganese

* 155 mg Omega-3 fatty acids

* 306 mg Omega-6 fatty acids

* Just 64 calories

Strawberries

Succulent sweet/tart strawberries (Fragaria X ananassa) are a world favorite. From the plant family Rosaceae, strawberries are native to Europe and classified as creeper plants. Individual strawberries are approximately 3 centimeters in diameter and weigh about 25 grams. For each 100-gram serving (four berries), we receive an amazing amount of nutrition on a calorie-for-calorie basis.

Perhaps the most notable phytochemical compounds found in strawberries are ellagic acid and anthocyanins, both proven beneficial for effectively combating neurological diseases, various cancers, general inflammation, and aging. Strawberries are also very healthy sources of B-complex Vitamins, as well as Vitamins A and E. Mineral-wise, strawberries offer healthy amounts of copper, manganese, potassium, fluorine, and iron. To add icing to the cake, strawberries are loaded up with polyphenolic antioxidant flavonoids like zeaxanthin, beta-carotene, and lutein.

And every 100-gram (4 berries) serving of raw, organic strawberries gifts your body with:

* Just 32 calories

* No fats, cholesterol or sodium

* 98% DV of Vitamin C

* 65 mg of Omega-3 fatty acids

* 90 mg of Omega-6 fatty acids

Tomatoes

One of nature's most healthful, versatile, and beloved creations, tomatoes (Lycopersicon esculentum) belong to the Nightshade plant family (Solanaceae). Native to Central America, tomatoes were cultivated by both the Aztecs and the Mayans. Tomatoes are positively full of beneficial phytochemicals that almost all other food sources simply do not have.

More specifically, tomatoes are rich in lycopene, an antioxidant bioflavonoid that acts with carotenoids to very effectively protect cellular structures throughout the body from free radical damage. Tomatoes have been shown to combat endometrial, pancreatic, lung, prostate, breast, and colon cancer. Lycopene has also been shown to boost the body's resistance against harmful UV rays that cause skin cancer.

Another superstar phytochemical in tomatoes is the flavonoid compound zeaxanthin. Zeaxanthin is well known in part for its ability to protect the eyes from ARMD (age-related macular disease). Low calorie tomatoes have no fat, cholesterol or sodium to worry about. Instead, they are naturally blessed with lots of vitamins, minerals, water, antioxidants, and fiber. What could be better?

Every 100-gram serving of raw, red tomatoes also provides:

* 26% DV of Vitamin C

* 20% DV of Vitamin A

* 12% DV of Vitamin K

* Healthy amounts of magnesium, iron, potassium, calcium, and manganese

* 1.5 grams of dietary fiber

* 22 calories

When you select fruits and vegetables to put into your Green Smoothie recipes, be versatile and bold in your experimentation! There is no limit and there are no rules to follow.

If you feel like you need a cleansing Green Smoothie, experiment with cranberries, asparagus, and collard greens (for instance). If you want to boost your immunity, you might blend up a Green Smoothie made from spinach, oranges, and pomegranate fruit. Use the recipes included in this book to get your own creative juices flowing, but remember that the final recipes are all up to you.

Listen to your body!

Selecting and Storing Fruits and Vegetables

Now that we have a better understanding about why Green Smoothies are such powerful, concentrated food source, and how they can help us to live healthier, happier lives, it's time to get into some delicious, ultimately nutritious Green Smoothie recipes! Of course, I am including some of my personal favorites, but also some that I feel are best for detox, best for energy, best anti-cancer, and so on.

However, before we get to the actual recipes, let's talk real quick about some common sense guidelines for selecting and storing your vegetables and fruits. While there's nothing fancy to learn, it does help to develop an organized approach to smoothie making. In the long run, helpful smoothie tips will save you time, energy, frustration, money, and more. I used to just throw all my produce items in the crisper compartment in my fridge and then prep them, one by one, as needed – and that seemed completely okay to me. Then, when I started getting into the smoothie lifestyle, I realized I was spending a lot of time in my kitchen performing repetitive actions like washing, prepping, and cleaning up. Over time, I've developed some simple and effective rules that have streamlined my Green Smoothie operations.

Tips for Selecting and Storing Green Smoothie Ingredients

1. Keep your produce purchasing decisions diverse by choosing in-season fruits and vegetables. Always be bold and experiment with new fruits and vegetables that you may have never even tried before. Giving your body a wide range of minerals, vitamins, phytonutrients, and other beneficial constituents is always best. In-season produce also is at top quality levels – and offers the best pricing. Remember to support your local organic farmers!

2. Keep track of how much produce you actually use and how much is wasted. Give some realistic thought to how much produce you and your family actually use for the period of time you are shopping for. Remember that fresh produce is best so don't space your shopping days too far apart.

3. Always inspect fruit and vegetables closely before purchasing. Look for signs of rot, under-ripeness, poor development, bruising, discoloration, malformation, and anything else that may grab a hold of your senses. Also, use your nose! Our noses are one of the best tools we have for determining what we should, or should not, eat.

4. Make sure the produce you choose is at least close to being optimally ripe. Fruits and vegetables are maximally nutritious when properly ripe – and maximizing nutrient levels are what Green Smoothies are all about! You can sometimes buy under-ripe produce and let it finish the ripening process at home. This saves an occasional trip to the grocery.

5. Develop a sincere understanding of just how important it is to choose organic produce whenever possible. Yes, in most cases, organic choices cost a little more. However, be aware of the vast nutritional and other health differences that result when a given fruit or vegetable is NOT repetitively doused in pesticides, herbicides, and other chemical concoctions. Natural plants were not meant to constantly combat all those chemicals. Doing so depletes nutrients, hinders proper development, and poisons the plant.

6. Keep produce stored in a cool and dry spot. If you have certain fruits or vegetables that are ripening too quickly, place those in the refrigerator. Remember that many produce items can be frozen, if needed and then used

later. When making Green Smoothies, frozen ingredients add coldness and fun!

7. Especially when some produce items are difficult to find, you can add diversity to your Green Smoothies by choosing 100% juices. It's best, of course, to use fresh, whole produce in your smoothies. However, in a pinch, 100% pure cranberry, pomegranate, cherry, carrot, blueberry, or other type of juice works out just fine. It's not always possible to get certain desired fruits and vegetables at your local market, but you can normally find a nice selection of available juices.

A special tip for storing Green Smoothie produce ingredients.

Here's one of my favorites: Using seal-tight plastic storage containers. I normally shop for produce twice each week. This keeps me loaded up with Green Smoothie ingredients without having my fridge overstuffed and unmanageable.

When I get home from the grocery, I clean all the fruits and vegetables that I'll be using for the next three or four days. Then, leaving them in whole form whenever possible, I place each separate type of produce in appropriately sized plastic storage containers – you know, like the Glad or Zip-Lock type. These containers are affordable versatile, stackable, and very easy to use.

Note that some cheap off-brand containers available at some dollar stores are not worth messing with! They are poorly made, don't seal properly, and should be avoided. Go for the name brands on these. It will save you money, effort, and frustration in the long run.

Now, with my produce washed, sorted, and placed in storage containers, I can simply put them in the fridge, all stacked nice and neat so they are readily available when it's smoothie-making time. That's when I just grab what I need for the smoothie at hand. I use the fresh, clean produce inside and then rinse the empty containers in the sink. Then, after a quick rinse of the blender, I'm done! From beginning to end, the Green Smoothie making process takes me only about five or six minutes, clean up included. Then, I'm walking away from a clean kitchen, nutrient-loaded Green Smoothie in hand. Oh yeah!

Keeping your fruits and vegetables clean, fresh, and ready will maximize your smoothie-making enjoyment while minimizing the work involved. After a while, you'll naturally develop your own short cuts. It becomes easier to determine just the right amounts of produce to buy at the store. In no time at all, you'll be a Green Smoothie Master – able to run the whole show with smoothness, efficiency – and much health and deliciousness!

Green Smoothie Recipes

The following Green Smoothie recipes all have at least a few things in common. They are all absolutely brimming with vital phytonutrients, including minerals, vitamins, flavonoids, antioxidants, and much more. Calorie for calorie, Green Smoothies are some of the most complete and wholesome food sources known to humans. They are truly difficult to beat as a food source, as medicines – and simply as mouth-watering treats!

While some of these recipes will be even more effective than others at providing specific health benefits, be assured that every Green Smoothie recipe is an amazing health miracle! Every recipe here and every recipe that you will undoubtedly create for yourself, will be immeasurably beneficial when it comes to preventing, treating, and reversing many adverse health conditions and diseases, including, but never limited to:

* Cancer

* Cardiovascular diseases

* Hypertension (high blood pressure)

* Atherosclerosis

* Osteoarthritis

* Stroke

* Diabetes

* Alzheimer's, Parkinson's and other neurological conditions

* High cholesterol

* Acne and other skin conditions

* Various inflammation-related conditions

It's true that daily Green Smoothies will make your family healthier, happier, and more vitally enduring. Good health begins in the home (even if you live alone) and it's so important to actively dedicate some time each day to practicing good health. Your body is the only one you will ever have. It's your responsibility and your privilege to take the best care of it that you can. Green Smoothies make taking care of your body deliciously simplistic.

Green Smoothie Preparation and Consumption Guidelines

Oh how I love Green Smoothies! I don't mean to sound weird, but I love selecting the ingredients for them. I love shopping for fresh, organic produce. I love washing the fruits and vegetables, getting them ready for storage before they're needed. I especially love placing the ingredients in the blender! Every time I do, I imagine the bits and pieces of the greens and fruits swirling around in the blender. I think about how this particular Green Smoothie is going to taste. Most importantly, I think, is the feeling that I know that drinking Green Smoothies makes me feel and absolutely loads my body up with powerful, healing nutrients desperately needed for me thrive. It's like there's some part of me that knows it is coming and longs for the next Green Smoothie! Anyway, before I go crazy talking about how much I love them, let's go over some very helpful preparation and consumption tips that will definitely enhance your Green Smoothie experiences.

Green Smoothie Preparation and Consumption Tips

The US is known as the world's most overfed and undernourished nation, experiencing a literal epidemic of obesity, stress, high blood pressure, heart disease, diabetes, cancer, and more. Yet almost every health condition can be very effectively treated with increased availability and absorption of nutrients, especially certain types of nutrients like antioxidants. When we take raw, organic greens and fruits and blend them up, we make them into food sources loaded with life-enhancing nutrients that are very easily absorbed.

Remember that Green Smoothies are best made in a blender. Food processors are not necessary because we don't need to completely emulsify the foods; we just want to liquefy them into their most delicious states! Some blenders (the really cheap ones) seem to get bogged down with daily blending duties, especially if the fruits and vegetables you're blending have a lot of seeds or other difficult-to-blend constituents.

Now, you can think about investing in a higher priced, faster-revved blender, but most common blenders do the trick just fine – at least until you burn them up! Then again, it's awfully nice to have that extra power, durability, and performance that comes with a higher priced blender.

Anyway, here are the basic steps for preparing Green Smoothies:

Tip #1: Start your days the Green Smoothie way!

First thing in the morning, make up enough Green Smoothie mix for your day. Yes, it's best to have a fresh batch each time, but making a day's worth all at once saves some time and work. My husband makes his own smoothie and I make mine. The kids aren't quite as dedicated to the lifestyle as we are, but they do make Green Smoothies regularly and I believe they will make even more as they age and realize just how important their health is. Anyway, I like to put mine in a travel mug for slow sippin' delight! Put the rest in the fridge, a cooler, or somewhere else that keeps things cold.

Tip #2: Green Smoothies are made for sippin', not chuggin'!

Slow sip your Green Smoothies for maximal nutrient absorption. Beginning in your mouth, make sure to mix each drink with saliva so that the digestion process can begin early and efficiently. The lock-tight lid on my travel mug makes it difficult for me to spill my smoothies in the car and that little mouth slit is just perfect for taking small sips, just like when you drink coffee. Because the Green Smoothie is locked in the travel mug, I can always swish it around to re-stir the ingredients if there's any settling going on.

Tip #3: Keep your Green Smoothie recipes simple!

I recommend that you keep most of your smoothie recipes simple, as in just the green leafy vegetable, the fruits and/or vegetables, water, and ice chips. Most times, when you add seeds, nuts, or powder supplements to the smoothies, it gives them a distasteful flavor and texture (at least to me). I prefer the natural, simple goodness of greens, fruits, vegetables, and purified water. Also, these items can slow down the efficiency and speed with which the nutrients are absorbed.

Tip #4: Smoothies are smoothies, meals are meals!

Enjoy your Green Smoothies by themselves, not as a beverage that accompanies a meal. Again, those extra food sources will mix with the smoothie and diminish your ability to easily assimilate the nutrients it's trying to offer you. As a rule of thumb, don't eat or drink anything (except water if you're thirsty) for 45 minutes before and after consuming a Green Smoothie. That will give your body the time it needs to utilize the best of what the smoothie provides.

Tip #5: Keep those green leafys diversified!

Even though I have a particular affinity to spinach, I always keep my choices between green leafy vegetables diverse. The reason why is because all greens have certain types of alkaloids in them. Now, these are in very small, unharmful amounts, but if you continually take in the same type of greens, then you are continually tasking in the same type of alkaloids, time and again. That can cause a buildup of that type of alkaloid and cause you serious health issues. So, simply choose different greens for your smoothies and eliminate that chance. It also helps you to develop an appreciation for all the different types of greens and exposes you to a maximum amount of different phytonutrients.

Rightfully so, many people seem to associate Green Smoothies with detoxification. Green Smoothies are wonderful food sources from every angle, including the fact that they provide us with plenty of natural detoxification substances. They provide plenty of other nutrients that help our immune systems, livers, kidneys, lymph nodes, and other detoxifying systems working in good order. The result is a powerful detoxification aid that will make your body feel more vibrant, strong, and agile!

Enjoy the following Green Smoothie recipes and remember that the best Green Smoothie combination is the one that you still haven't concocted yet. Again, I recommend that you boldly experiment with loads of different ingredients - and always enjoy drinking in the wonderful world of Green Smoothie health!

Cranberry-Based Green Smoothie Recipes

Cranberry Citrus Dandelion Green Smoothie for Detoxification

By far, the biggest question I am asked is, "What type of Green Smoothie is good for detox?" Well, I'm going to start out the 51 Green Smoothie recipes with my favorite detoxification Green Smoothie. It's a lovely mixture that combines the powers of dandelions, cranberries, citrus, and water. Drink one of these Green Smoothies any time you feel blah, down, or otherwise crappy. Your body won't be able to do anything, but react enthusiastically and thankfully!

Detoxification is a subject that everyone needs to address in their lives. We are exposed to so many toxins in our everyday lives. It's actually stunning. Toxins in the air, in the water, in the soil, and just about everywhere else are constantly bombarding us, forcing us to protect ourselves, even and especially at a cellular level.

Our livers and kidneys are overburdened. They need our help! It's so refreshing and revitalizing to enjoy regular servings of powerful detoxifying Green Smoothies. When you add in all the antioxidants and other phytonutrients that this Cranberry Citrus Dandelion recipe contains, you are concocting one seriously potent source of dietary superiority!

Be aware (if you don't already know) that dandelions are bitter. They are definitely an acquired taste. That's why the banana is added to the recipe; it helps to tame down some of that dandelion bitterness. If you just can't hack the dandelion taste, you can still make a mean detoxification Green Smoothie by substituting fresh baby spinach for the dandelion. There's no bitterness there – and still an obscene amount of antioxidizing, detoxifying phytonutrients!

I love to help my body get cleansed of disease-causing toxins!

Dandelion greens are absolutely delicious in their own ways. I really like them a lot, but that wasn't quite true right away. It helps me to step outside my normal thought patterns and truly try to experience and appreciate new natural tastes for what they are. In the case of dandelion greens, I remind myself that they are loaded with wholesome goodness that's helping me to be a more vital, effective, and happy person. When I look at things that way, I love the taste!

Dandelion greens are considered by many to be the best green leafy vegetable for detoxification purposes. I agree. They are very good sources for calcium, antioxidants, iron, and more. Cranberries are known worldwide for their antioxidant properties, making them strong immune system boosters. Then there's the cinnamon, orange, lime, and banana added in to make this a smooth, unique and very effective cleansing Green Smoothie. Enjoy one regularly!

Cranberry Citrus Dandelion Green Smoothie

3/4 cup of fresh (or frozen) cranberries

2 cups dandelion greens

1 orange

Juice of 1/2 lime

2 small frozen bananas, cut in quarters

1/2 to 3/4 cup purified water

Ice chips to suit

Again, I would start with the dandelion greens and some of the water and give them a 15 or 20-second head start on the other ingredients. Then add in the rest of the ingredients and blend until smooth and creamy to suit your preferences. (I like lots of ice blended in mine – like an icee!)

These extra-nutritious low-fat detox Green Smoothies contain about 340 calories, more than 7 grams of protein, over 15 grams of fiber, and tons of other amazingly healthy constituents!

Raspberry-Based Green Smoothie Recipes

There are three Green Smoothie recipes that I absolutely love and I want to start off with them. Actually, one of them is my son's favorite, but I still love it anyway! Raspberries are the central ingredient for these first three Green Smoothie recipes. That's because raspberries are naturally unique in appearance, structure, taste, nutrients, and power! I crave the tart/sweet flavor of raspberries and love the taste that's created by mixing them with spinach. (I choose spinach often because it's my favorite green leafy to begin with and it has a mild taste that never overpowers the smoothies.)

Remember that raspberries are especially rich in flavonoid compounds like tannins, ellagic acid, anthocyanins, catechins, and more. They give us healthy doses of both Omega-3 and Omega-6 fatty acids, as well as strong amounts of Vitamins C, fiber, manganese, copper, iron, and magnesium. 100 grams of raspberries has about 65 calories.

Spinach is my favorite green leafy vegetable for several reasons. First, I love Popeye (always did as a kid and still do)! It always gets me riled up inside when Popeye breaks out a can of spinach and gobbles it down. The power that results comes from the fact that spinach is absolutely packed full of empowering nutrients, including 110% DV of Vitamin K, 377% DV of Vitamin A, and 84% DV of manganese. It's practically calorie-free and has no cholesterol or fats to worry about.

Remember that it's completely okay to switch your greens up as you like. If you want collards instead of spinach, go for it! If you choose chard over bok choy, so be it! There will be just a few nutritional differences between the different greens, but all green leafy vegetables are wonderfully healthful and delicious. Different greens do have very different tastes so experiment to find your favorite combinations.

For the first of these three raspberry/spinach based Green Smoothies, I'm going to throw in some succulent mango fruit. One hundred grams of mango adds such a wonderful flavor and texture to the mix that it's my top pick of all smoothies, period.

Mango fruit adds about 70 calories to this mix, as well as another 46% DV of Vitamin C, 156 mg of potassium, and life-enhancing amounts of carotene-alpha, carotene-beta, and zeaxanthin. This raspberry/mango/spinach Green

Smoothie is a completely miraculous food source that tastes better than just about anything I can even imagine.

Raspberry Mango Spinach Green Smoothie

2 cups fresh spinach

1 cup raspberries

1 medium to large mango

About 3/4 cup of water

Ice chips to suit

I start out with the spinach and water, blending for about 20 seconds in a high speed blender. Then, I throw in the raspberries and mango fruit. I blend another 30 to 45 seconds, adding ice chips thrown in the hole at the top of the blender container's lid. I add the ice chips because I like my smoothies extra cold and refreshing. While the blending is finishing up, I grab a frosted glass from the freezer and have it ready. A quick pour and I'm in nutritional heaven!

Each Raspberry Mango Spinach Green Smoothie provides you with just about:

* 225 calories

* Obscene amounts of Vitamins K, A, and C

* More than 6 grams of protein

* 59 grams of carbohydrates

* 1.5 grams of healthy fats

* Loads of minerals

* Various antioxidant phytonutrient compounds

My other personal favorite raspberry-based Green Smoothie recipe contains both blackberries and bananas. Once again, I prefer spinach for this one, mainly because of its mild taste. In fact, to be completely honest with you, I probably should mix my greens up more than I do. I just really like spinach and it's so perfectly healthy that I just stick with it – probably like 75% of the time! I'm in no way recommending that to you – just being honest.

Blackberries add in even more of those pigment based antioxidants, as well as extra doses of Vitamin A, C, E, and more. Who doesn't love the mild yet flavorful and healthful impact of bananas in their smoothies? Bananas also add that one-of-a-kind creamy texture to beverages. (For an even smoother version of this Green Smoothie, throw in 1/4 cup of fresh avocado.) Raspberries, blackberries, spinach, and bananas when mixed together create a succulent, refreshing, and energizing delicacy!

Raspberry Blackberry Banana Spinach Green Smoothie

2 cups fresh spinach

1 large banana

1 cup raspberries

1 cup blackberries

1/2 to 3/4 cup water

Ice chips to suit

Each Raspberry Blackberry Banana Spinach Smoothie contains about 280 calories, 6 grams of protein, 53 grams of carbohydrates, 12% DV of calcium, as well as loads of Vitamins A and C.

Raspberry Apple Kale Green Smoothie

Apples are one of the world's most famous fruits. They are extra tasty, juicy, and full of healthy nutrients that help us to thrive! Combining apples and raspberries just seems so natural to me. These two flavors complement one another very well, creating a taste sensation that is bold, crisp, and just a bit on the exotic side. Then, when the kale is added into the mix, the result is a vitality-increasing "Super Food" that tastes absolutely excellent!

Isothiocyanates, flavonoids, carotenoids, glucosinolates, plenty of vitamins, minerals, and more are all included in every medley healthy serving of kale. Its taste is not overpowering, but offers a beautiful texture and color to enjoy. Here's what to blend:

1 cup kale

1 cup raspberries

3 medium apples (I throw the entire apples in!)

1/2 to 3/4 cup purified water

Ice chips to suit

Each Raspberry Apple Kale Green Smoothie contains about 285 calories, more than 5 grams of protein, 64 grams of carbohydrates, only 1.4 grams of fat, more than 1400% DV of Vitamin K, and so much more.

Tomato-Based Green Smoothie Recipes

A lot of my students react like I've shot them when I start talking about how much I love tomato-based Green Smoothies. For some reason, I seem to meet quite a few people who feel that tomatoes don't belong in a Green Smoothies recipe. They think that Green Smoothies are all about sweet, fruity fruits. Well, tomatoes happen to rock in Green Smoothies. They're some of my favorite recipes because even though we take tomatoes for granted a lot because they're so commonly available in many forms, they are still some of the healthiest foods in existence. I love tomatoes and I'm proud of it!

When you take a minute to think about what flavor combinations go well with tomatoes, you can come up with some extra-delicious and mega-nutritious concoctions! Here are three of my personal favorite tomato-based Green Smoothie recipes for you to try when you want something unique, refreshing, and extra healthy:

Tomato Garlic Spinach Green Smoothie

Three Super Foods in one delicious source – introducing the Tomato Garlic Spinach Green Smoothie. This is one of my absolute favorites and it figures because I am crazy about all three ingredients in any form: raw, steamed, baked, grilled, in salads, sautéed, you name it - I love tomatoes, garlic, and spinach! Now granted, I do not often go around crunching on raw garlic. However, I really, really like garlic in just about everything I cook – at least some garlic powder! You could definitely say that I am a Garlic Freak!

All three of these foods are absolutely amazing in terms of their potential medicinal usages. They are multi-talented vitality advancers that can yield extra-strong health benefits in your life! It's true that when you cross tomatoes, garlic, and spinach in a Green Smoothie recipe, the result is a *muy delicioso* beverage that contains:

1. Mega doses of flavonoid antioxidants from the spinach

2. Cancer-smashing lycopene from the tomatoes

3. Immune system enhancing thiosulfinates, sulfoxides, and dithiins from the garlic

This is serious medicine folks!

When I first drank one of these, I thought I had transcended the boundaries of this planet and found nutritional heaven. I was truly impressed with the blast of health that I delivered to my body in such a tasteful, natural, and powerful style. I still love every last sip of every Tomato Garlic Spinach Green Smoothie I make. In fact, I love these so much that I put the "power-sip" on the empty glass after I've consumed the contents. I don't even care (too much) about the slurping sounds I'm very likely to make! Anyway, here are the ingredients:

1 big, ripe, raw tomato

2 cups spinach

Garlic to taste (I use about 4 separate cloves, mmm mmm!)

1/2 to 3/4 cup purified water

Ice chips to suit

Tomato Asparagus Chard Green Smoothie

Continuing on with the tomato theme, the Tomato Asparagus Chard Green Smoothie is a total taste star in my opinion. It has depth and flavor that make me truly appreciate the health that's being delivered to me. I actually feel blessed every time I drink any Green Smoothie. That's because I know how many people there are on the planet that don't have any means to such a delightful, nutrient-packed food source. It also makes me think of all those who do have the option to feed themselves healthily, but simply choose not to.

Anyway, here are the ingredients for the Tomato Asparagus Green Smoothie:

2 cups kale or spinach

2 medium ripe tomatoes

1/2 bunch of asparagus (about 1 cup)

1 stalk celery

Purified water and ice chips to suit

Call me crazy, but I'd rather have a juicy, sweet Green Smoothie every time rather than a deep fried bunch of French fries and a greasy hamburger!

Spicy Tomato Jalapeno Green Smoothie

Remember to experiment with your Green Smoothie recipes. Tomatoes go very well with all greens – and then adding in items like garlic, asparagus, and so many others makes the tastes even better! For instance, two of my other favorite vegetables to mix with tomatoes in a Green Smoothie are green peppers and jalapeno peppers. I love spicy foods and I love spicy Green Smoothies. Try the following recipe out on a day when you're feeling a bit bold. You'll enjoy this not-too-spicy Green Smoothie that's bursting with antioxidants, vitamins, minerals – and bunches of exciting flavor!

2 cups kale, chard, or spinach

2 large tomatoes

1 whole jalapeno pepper (steamed for 5 minutes before blending to soften)

1/2 green pepper (steamed along with the jalapeno pepper)

Purified water and ice chips to suit

Remember that Green Smoothie aren't all about sweet fruits like pineapples, bananas, and mangoes. Tomatoes make one of the best and most healthful Green Smoothies bases there are. Experiment and come up with your own tomato-based Green Smoothies!

Green Smoothie Pudding Recipes

Who in their right mind doesn't like pudding? Well, in my house, pudding is received like water in the desert – we all crave it! The following recipes are delicious spins on what we traditionally think of as pudding, but they're extra creamy, super sweet, and totally yummy – they just happen to be loaded with phytonutrients instead of sugar. Try these out on babies, small children, teens, college students, middle-aged adults, and grandparents. Everybody loves pudding!

Exotic Citrus Green Smoothie Pudding

Sometimes you may want to change things up a bit. Try this Green Smoothie pudding recipe. Its creamy texture will please your tongue while its nutrients deliver a boatload of goodness to your body and brain. It's like eating super-healthy pudding! While the ingredients below list 1 cup of purified water, make sure you judge this as you are blending. Sometimes, I put just a little too much water in and end up with runny pudding – and nobody likes runny pudding!

The tastes that come together in this delicious pudding are perfectly suited for each other. This pudding also makes truly dynamite baby, toddler, teenager, and adult food – everyone loves it! If anything, just try out a batch and don't even mention that it's healthy. Just let each family member try it without saying a word. Nine times out of ten, they will swear how much they love it – and ask for more. Here's what to blend:

1 cup pineapple fruit

1 cup fresh parsley

1 Abbot (if available) pear

5 grape leaves

1 medium peeled orange

1 cup purified water (added slowly for desired consistency)

I'll tell you what: if your family (or just you!) likes the Green Pudding above, then you should also try out this next recipe for unique, mouth-watering persimmon pudding.

Persimmon Green Pudding

3 seeded, peeled persimmons

2 cups baby spinach

1 ripe banana

1 cup purified water (used with caution again)

Quick Pineapple Green Smoothie Recipes

These pineapple-based Green Smoothie recipes are very straightforward and don't have long lists of ingredients – precisely why they are so naturally, simplistically delicious. Sweet, yet tangy, juicy pineapples are scientifically called Ananas comosus and belong to the Bromeliaceae family of plants. One of the most beautiful things about pineapples is that they contain a unique phytonutrient enzyme called bromelain. It is made up primarily of protein-digesting (proteolytic) enzymes that are known to do a couple of really impressive things inside your body.

1. Decrease excessive blood coagulation (clotting) associated with chronic inflammation.

2. Inhibit the development of tumor cells.

Of course, there are many other wonderful reasons to love pineapples like the fact that they taste like a juicy, sweet/tart tropical heaven. I sincerely love pineapples! They provide high amounts of manganese, Vitamins B1 (thiamine), B6 (pyridoxine), C, and they have loads of other very valuable nutrients as well. Not to mention that they are one of those fruits that look alien like they are from another world! Well, I wanted to include a triple recipe section for the pineapple – just because they are so delicious and exotic. So here we go!

Pineapple Mango Green Smoothie

As you know, I am a huge mango fan, and I just love the taste of a cold, r ,
mango! When you take the beautiful character of a mango and mix it with
the natural goodness of spinach and pineapple, the result is truly delicious.
Try this recipe icy cold on a hot day!

2 cups fresh baby spinach

1 cup fresh pineapple fruit

1 large, ripe mango

3/4 to 1 cup purified water and ice chips to suit

Basic and refreshing, each serving of this Green Smoothie will supply your
body with only 200 calories, less than 1 gram of fat, more than 4 grams of
protein, and 57 grams of carbohydrates.

Orange Green Smoothie

es are rich in Vitamin C and serve as natural antioxidants. distinct taste that is undeniably classy. I personally like an ist a bit tart. Super sweet oranges are great for eating, but rtness adds character to an already sweet Green Smoothie like this one. The banana in this recipe adds the creamy texture that is so popular in the Green Smoothie world. You can use any greens you choose. I find that baby spinach works very well with the pineapple-based recipes so I stick with that. Here's what to put in the blender:

2 cups organic baby spinach

1 cup fresh pineapple

Seedless fruit from 1 large orange

1 large banana

1/2 to 3/4 cup purified water as needed

Ice chips to suit

This tropical, delicious Green Smoothie provides about 300 calories per serving, less than 1 gram of fat, almost 6 grams of protein, and a whopping 70 grams of carbohydrates.

Pineapple Banana Green Smoothie

There are very few, if any fruits that bananas do not go along with in a taste sense. Bananas are so versatile and offer their own long list of holistic health benefits. They also have that special texture, making each Green Smoothie recipe come out creamy with a smooth consistency. I quite simply combine bananas with succulent pineapple to create a powerhouse, energizing drink loaded with healthy phytonutrients, including of course, loads of antioxidants! Mix the following ingredients until creamy smooth and delicious.

1½ cups pineapple

3 large, ripe bananas

2 cups fresh baby spinach

Purified water and ice chips to suit

My husband actually likes to throw one vine-ripened tomato into this recipe. He says it's fab! However, prepared as above, this Green Smoothie offers your body just about 300 calories along with 6 grams of protein, 79 grams of carbohydrates, only 1 gram of fat, very little sodium or cholesterol, and loads of other healthy constituents. Enjoy regularly for best results!

Kiwi-Based Green Smoothie Recipes

Kiwis are one of the most interesting and exotic fruits in the world. They are Chinese natives and offer us nutritional advantages. They're uniquely delectable and naturally loaded with Vitamins C, A, K, and E. Kiwis also contain significant amounts of magnesium, iron, potassium, and other important minerals. Of course, kiwis are a good sources of the healthy Omega-3 and Omega-6 fatty acids. They are fiber-rich, full of antioxidants, and low in fat, sodium, cholesterol, and calories.

Kiwi Strawberry Spinach Green Smoothie

Like peaches and kale, few produce blended couples that are ¹
than strawberries and kiwis. It's like nature intends for these tw˰
to be enjoyed together. My husband and I think of these smoothies like
candy! They are so sweet and tasty that my mouth actually waters just
thinking of them! We make sure to serve them in raw sugar-lined, frozen
glasses to make the experience more enjoyable. We make and drink
smoothies every day, but once in a while, we like to go all out and get
romantic with it! It's a fun, delicious, and feel-good way to be healthier!

Kiwi Strawberry Baby Spinach Green Smoothies are naturally packed with all
the nutrients we need to initiate a major health blast inside our bodies.
Remember that strawberries are famous for their ellagic acid and
anthocyanin content. They help us avoid neurological disease, cancer,
generalized inflammation, and much more. The kiwis kick in the exotic
flavor and texture and the baby spinach adds in mountains of health. The
result is a super-tasteful, energizing, and life-enhancing complete food
source that you'll look forward to drinking. Why not make it special with a
crystal-clear, sugary, frosted serving glass?

Try this recipe and you'll see what I mean!

2 kiwis

1 cup strawberries

2 cups baby spinach

1/2 to 3/4 cup purified water

Ice chips to suit

This succulent, smooth (and romantic!) delicacy will keep you looking and
feeling sexy with only 148 calories, less than 2 grams of healthy fats, almost
5 grams of protein, 36 grams of carbohydrates, very low sodium and

olesterol, and so many nutrients that you'll feel empowered instantly upon consumption!

Kiwi Banana Mint Green Smoothie

When I first tried this combination, I was a bit reserved. This was actually my teenage son's idea. He loves anything minty, as well as bananas. We had an overstock of kiwis because I found a bunch marked down just at the right time when I was at the grocery. Anyway, I was pressing kiwis that day and he was bent on mint so the kiwi, banana, and mint combo was born. In a nutshell, it is delicious! The doggone kid was right! The mint and banana create a flavor that's just out of this world and the texture is very nice too. Kale has always been the choice green for this smoothie – I'm not sure why, but it just seems to go right with the mint I think.

Health wise, the kiwis, bananas, and spinach are a natural blessing already, but the mint leaves add even more! Spearmint belongs to the plant family called lamiaceae and is scientifically known as Mentha spicata. It's less scientifically known as common mint and/or garden mint. Spearmint plants are branching perennial herbs native to the Mediterranean. With plenty of essential oil and menthol components, spearmint is also packed with vitamins, minerals, and powerful phytonutrients. It's a commonly used planet for various health benefits including:

* Headaches

* Fatigue

* Asthma

* Bronchitis

* Stress

* Nausea

* Dermatitis

Spearmint also contains healthy levels of linalool, carvone, alpha-pinene, beta-pinene, caryophyllene, limonene, cineole, and more that are known to combat fatigue and stress. Spearmint also supplies extra doses of potassium, calcium, iron, manganese, magnesium, and other minerals. Spearmint can help us to metabolize our foods more efficiently, synthesize hemoglobin, control our heart rate, and moderate blood pressure. Spearmint also happens to contain a variety of antioxidants, including beta-carotene, Vitamin C, folates, Vitamin B6, riboflavin, thiamine, and more.

Kiwi Banana Mint Kale Green Smoothie Recipe

2 kiwis

1 large banana

2 cups raw kale

4 spearmint leaves

1/2 to 3/4 cup purified water

Ice chips to suit

Now that's a healthy food source! Each serving you drink will flood your body with heavy nutrition, all with just about 225 calories, 1 gram of fat, more than 5 grams of protein, and a sustaining 56 grams of carbohydrates.

Kiwi Orange Swiss Chard Green Smoothie

To me, this is one of the more exotic Green Smoothie recipes, not just because it's so unusual, but because it gives me a feeling of sophistication and loftiness. There's something about slow-sipping this delicious Green Smoothie that makes me feel like a superstar! The kiwi is an exotic tasting fruit with a smooth texture. It mixes so very well with orange – and the Swiss chard brings it all together with smooth, delicate flavors.

Health wise, we all know that oranges are naturally high in the antioxidant Vitamin C and they also have a lot of other blessings for our bodies. Oranges are from the plant family, Rutaceae and are botanically named Citrus sinensis. All types are delicious, including Persian, Navel, Valencia, Blood ,and many others.

The segments of orange fruit are called carpels. They're made up of separate fluid vesicles. Oranges are excellent sources of dietary fiber, pectin and a plentiful variety of other nutrients as well. Remember that pectin is the natural laxative that protects the mucous membranes inside the colon. They do this by decreasing the exposure time of the colon to toxic substances. Pectin also binds to cancerous cells and transports them out of the body. It also helps to significantly, yet naturally, regulate blood-glucose levels.

Two of the most noted flavonoid phytonutrients found in oranges are hesperetin and narigenin. Both are classified as effective antioxidants. They exhibit anti-inflammatory effects and are shown to decrease oxidative damage to DNA. Oranges also contain the antioxidants Vitamin A, alpha and beta-carotene, zeaxanthin, beta-cryptoxanthin, lutein, and more. Of course, they're also loaded with other goodies like thiamine, pyridoxine, and folate. Here's what to put in the blender:

2 kiwis

1 large orange (seeds or no seeds, up to you!)

2 cups Swiss chard

1/2 to 3/4 cup of purified water

Ice chips to suit

Ultra-smooth and totally succulent, kiwis add a lot of excitement and nutrition to your Green Smoothie recipes. Make sure to keep experimenting with different flavor and nutrient combinations to maximize the benefits you'll receive!

Creamy, Rich Avocado-Based Green Smoothies

Avocados are another fruit that makes me feel mysterious and classy. They are so original and unique! Loaded with good fats like Omega-3 fatty acids, an avocado is a superior survival food! The following Green Smoothie recipes will finish out thick, creamy, and very rich. These smoothies also have more caloric value than most others, right around 400 calories per serving.

Believe me, these Green Smoothies are exceptional nutritional storehouses that treat your body to uncountable health benefits every single time you enjoy one. That's another beautiful thing about Green Smoothies - they actually are so naturally delicious that it is a real treat to sip them. Enjoy these avocado-based Green Smoothie recipes any time you want something sweet, creamy, and richly satisfying!

Avocado Apple Green Smoothie

2 cups raw kale

1 Granny Smith apple

1/2 avocado

1 tablespoon lime juice

Purified water and ice chips to suit

Each serving will provide you with about 350 calories, 3 grams of protein, 15 grams of good fats, and 27 grams of carbohydrates.

Avocado Banana Green Smoothie

With these avocado-based Green Smoothie recipes, I don't like using a lot of water. Of course, you have to make it so that it is liquidly smooth and drinkable, but I personally like to keep the consistency thick and serve them ice cold in a frosted glass! Here's what to blend up for an ultra-tasty Avocado Banana Green Smoothie:

2 cups Swiss chard

1/2 avocado

2 large, ripe bananas

1 stalk celery

Purified water and ice chips to suit

Every mouth-watering serving of these Avocado Banana Green Smoothies will fortify your body with about 375 calories, 5 grams of protein, 16 grams of healthy fats, and more than 60 grams of carbohydrates.

Avocado Kiwi Green Smoothie

Avocados and kiwis go together wonderfully! They come together to create a one-of-a-kind taste experience that's absolutely plentiful in nutritional value. This is another of those Green Smoothie recipes that makes my mouth water just thinking of it. There's definitely an element of sophistication in a food source like this. Once again, I'm left speechless as I try to imagine any reason at all why every human on the planet doesn't commit to the Green Smoothie lifestyle! Oh well, at least we see the obvious truths, huh? Okay, here's what to blend for an exotic tasting Avocado Kiwi Green Smoothie:

2 cups fresh baby spinach

1/2 avocado

2 kiwis

Purified water and ice chips to suit

Every health-packed serving of this recipe yields about 370 calories, 16 grams of fat, 63 grams of carbohydrates, and more than 6 grams of protein.

Avocado Blackberry Green Smoothie

This Green Smoothie recipe doesn't have any fantastic story attached to it. I was just thinking of something that would go well with avocado one day. I thought that just about everything goes well with avocado, but what I decided to use was blackberries because I had some that needed to be used. Since I made the first one, I've loved them. These are SO tasty and rich. They're absolutely delicious, super nutritious, and just plain fun to make for the family. Here's what to put in the blender:

2 cups kale or baby spinach

1/2 avocado

1 cup blackberries

Purified water and ice chips to suit

Simple, direct, and to the point, these avocado Green Smoothie recipes will be instant hits in any setting you serve them. Trust me, I know! Each serving will give you about 375 calories, 16 grams of healthy fats, over 6 grams of protein, and 53 grams of carbohydrates.

Green Smoothie Applesauce Recipes

Classic Green Smoothie Applesauce

Like the Green Smoothie puddings listed earlier, Green Smoothie applesauce is a delicacy loaded with phytonutrients. Served cold, it's an excellent, healthy treat for people of all ages and tastes. When blending this applesauce, make sure to add the water in slowly to control the consistency. Like runny pudding, nobody likes runny applesauce! Likewise, be cautious with the cinnamon, as it can become overpowering quickly. After you make this a few times, you'll hone your recipe to fit your family's tastes and they will always receive it as a nice treat!

4 large apples (I choose Granny Smith)

1 medium banana

2 cups baby spinach

1/3 to 1/2 teaspoon cinnamon

1 to 1½ cups purified water

Blend until well mixed and desired consistency is achieved. Remember to let your applesauce get good and cold before serving. It's so good!

Jaded Apple Applesauce

Here's another variety to try out. It's called Jaded Apple Applesauce and it pumps up your body with incredible nutrients while simultaneously sending love signals to your taste buds. These Green Smoothies truly are simple to make. Clean up is quick and easy. Your family will appreciate the thoughtfulness you show when you make this for them. Use the following ingredients:

5 Granny Smith apples (or whatever type you prefer)

1 bunch fresh, organic parsley

1/2 inch ginger root

That's it! Just blend it until you achieve the desired consistency and you'll have a healthy, fun dessert for the family (or a decadent snack for yourself!)

Peach-Based Green Smoothie Recipes

I love peaches! Especially when those perfectly ripe peaches are just so juicy and uniquely delicious. They are also wonderfully versatile in terms of their ability to blend nicely with other flavors. In fact, it's difficult for me to think of any type of fruit, vegetable, or even meat, that a peach doesn't go along with. That's probably why peach-based Green Smoothies are some of my favorites. They're totally mouth-watering, loaded with healthy ingredients, and 100% enjoyable!

Remember that peaches offer us some unique health gifts like heavy doses of the antioxidants lutein, zeaxanthin, Vitamin C, cryptoxanthin-beta, lycopene, carotene-beta, and others. Peaches are also high in fiber, B-complex Vitamins, and potassium. Peaches also have a fluid, creamy texture that makes a really nice base for Green Smoothies.

The first peach Green Smoothie recipe mixes in America's favorite berry, the strawberry! There's a healthy serving of – you guessed it – baby spinach! Here's what to mix in the blender:

Peach Strawberry Spinach Green Smoothie

2 whole medium to large peaches, fully ripe

6 fresh strawberries

2 cups baby spinach (or your choice of leafy greens)

About 1/2 cup purified water

Ice chips to suit

That's it – all you need to make a super-healthy, antioxidant-loaded Green Smoothie that's all the way tasty! Each one provides you with just about 140 calories, 5 grams of protein, 32 grams of carbohydrates, almost zero fat, a long list of vitamins, minerals, and phytonutrients.

Straight Peach Kale Green Smoothie

You may not believe me, but peaches and kale go together like few other natural gifts – absolutely lip-smackin'! I make a Peach-Kale Green Smoothie as a standby when I'm feeling indecisive. I know that it offers maximum health benefits. I know it tastes totally delicious. I know that it's light and low-cal. It pumps up my strength and rewards me for staying strong and vital. Try it out. It's fast and fun!

2 cups raw kale

1 large pitted peach

1/2 to 3/4 cup purified water

Ice chips to suit

It couldn't be easier! Just throw the ingredients in the blender and blend until smooth. This Green Smoothie is simple, quick, and so tasty! Trust me, you'll love it.

Peach Avocado Carrot Green Smoothie

Peaches, avocados, and carrots make such nice compliments to one another, especially when mixed with some tender, fresh baby spinach! This smoothie has a subtle, mild taste that leaves a thick, very enjoyable aftertaste. Just blend the following for about 55 seconds at high speed:

1 large pitted peach

1 shredded carrot (Hint – purchase your fresh shredded carrots in re-sealable bags)

1/3 avocado

2 cups baby spinach

1/2 to 3/4 cup purified water

Ice chips to suit

You see? Quick, simple and delicious! Every Peach Avocado Carrot Green Smoothie contains just about 225 calories, 8 grams of healthy fats, 6 grams of protein, 54 grams of carbohydrate, and extra-high doses of various nutrients.

Other Green Smoothie Recipes

Bitter Love Green Smoothie

Aloe Vera, chard, banana, and chickweed sounds like love to me!
Sometimes love can be bitter, but this type of bitter isn't bad at all. In fact,
it's Vitamin-loaded, mineral-packed, phytonutrient-full, and really tasty as
well. This healing Green Smoothie is a mix of some of the healthiest plants
known to mankind – and you'll definitely feel the vibrant differences every
serving will make in your days. Put these ingredients in your blender and
blend until well-mixed:

1 large leaf of aloe vera (with skin intact)

1 cup Swiss chard

3 cups chickweed

1 banana

Fruit of 1 peach

Fruit of 1 pear

1/3 to 1/2 cup of purified water

Ice chips to suit

My Cucumber Love Green Smoothie

Who doesn't love a ripe, juicy cucumber, especially on a hot summer day? This simple Green Smoothie recipe can be used as one of those straightforward, simple-to-make Green Smoothie delights that can be used as a quick standby for indecisiveness. It's fast and furious like few other food sources in existence and it will help your body to heal, cleanse, and thrive! With every serving, your body gets energized, detoxified and fortified in extra-high degrees. Just blend the following until you get the desired texture and taste you crave:

1 entire bunch of dandelion greens

1 large cucumber

2 to 3 cups purified water

Ice chips to suit

The Balanced Life Green Smoothie

To me, enjoying life has a lot to do with how balanced you are, how well you maintain your life's challenges, and how well you manage your emotions. It's highly important to me to optimize each day with results that I can see and be proud of. Of course, there are days when I accomplish next to nothing, but hey, we all have those days right? However, most of the time, it's my goal to stay active and get things done.

I also happen to know that getting things done and done well has a lot to do with how well you feel. If your body and/or brain are dragging, then you're going to be less effective and less successful - that's a no-no! So, we have to balance our lives efficiently and sometimes, a bit regimentally. Making Green Smoothies a part of daily life will certainly help you along the road to finding balance. Green Smoothies give your body the nutrients and fuel it needs to thrive and accomplish the goals that you set for yourself.

That brings me to this next Green Smoothie recipe: The Balanced Life Green Smoothie. It's very basic without a long list of ingredients to complicate things and to throw them off balance. It's so deliciously natural and simplistic, you'll agree that it will be an instant classic the second you touch your lips to it! Just blend:

1 cup fresh kale

Fruit of 1 large mango

1 cup purified water

Ice chips to suit

The above ingredients when blended will yield about one quart of Green Smoothie. I encourage you to blend up one of these right away and taste how sweet and refreshing it is. This basic Green Smoothie will add energy to your day, clarity to your thoughts, and bring all-important balance to your life. Enjoy!

Orange Purple Yellow Green Smoothie

Orange carrots, purple beets, yellow pears, and green spinach get together for a party in your frosted glass in the Orange Purple Yellow Green Smoothie! Loads of color, loads of flavor, loads of nutrients, and loads of fun, these Green Smoothies please just about everyone. It always amazes me that most people concede that Green Smoothies taste pretty good and are fairly healthy. The truth is that Green Smoothies taste EXCELLENT – and they contain more vital nutrients than every other food source imaginable! This smoothie will deliver so many antioxidants, vitamins, minerals, and decadence to your day that it's just difficult to fathom. One word of caution - be careful with the beet juice! It stains like crazy and very difficult to remove, if possible at all. Other than that, blend it well and serve it cold to enjoy all those healthy benefits in super-tasty style!

1 cup of spinach

1/2 cup of beet

1 medium carrot

(Note that a 10-minute steam on the beets and carrots will soften them and make the Green Smoothie more enjoyable without sacrificing nutrients)

1 fresh pear

2 tablespoons organic lemon juice, freshly squeezed of course

2 teaspoons minced ginger root

About 2 cups purified water

Ice chips to suit

Every time you enjoy a delicious serving of Orange Purple Yellow Green Smoothie, you provide your body with just about 125 calories, zero fat, zero cholesterol, 2 grams of protein, 7 grams of fiber, and 35 grams of carbohydrates. Enjoy these low-cal multi-colored smoothies any time you need a true blast of energizing nutrition in your day!

Jet Fuel Green Smoothie

This next Green Smoothie is what my son calls "Jet Fuel." It has several ingredients (not really my style), but blends together in a smooth, succulent style. It tastes *muy delicioso*, but is a little busy for me personally. By now, you should know a little about me. I like to keep my Green Smoothies raw, simple, and specialized. However, Jet Fuel is an amazing mixture of health-loaded ingredients and so I absolutely love it when my son starts gathering ingredients for the blend. He swears that these Green Smoothie powerhouses make him feel on top of the world. He seems to energize even as he's drinking them. Maybe it's a placebo for him, but he seems to get mighty wired! Here's what to use:

1 cup red lettuce

1 small aloe vera leaf

2 ripe kiwis

1 seedless, peeled orange

1 cup seedless red grapes

1½ cups purified water

Ice chips to suit

Sun Salutation Green Smoothie

I've been practicing yoga for more than fifteen years now (another secret to balancing life's mishaps and maintaining balance). In yoga, there is a famous asana (pose) routine called the Sun Salutation. I've named this Green Smoothie after the Sun Salutation because this is my favorite early morning Green Smoothie. It's light, refreshing, energizing, ultra-healthy, and tastes like an exotic delicacy. Place the following in your blender:

1 cup chopped dandelion greens

2 stalks celery

½ inch piece of ginger, chopped

2 ripe peaches

1 cup pineapple fruit

1/2 to 3/4 cup purified water

Ice chips to suit

You'll absolutely love the way that this yoga-based Green Smoothie makes you feel. It's the perfect way to start your morning. I personally love going out on the back deck and looking at the trees, animals, and nature while sipping mine. It's a beautiful beginning to the day and makes it difficult to get off to a bad start!

Black & Blue Berry Bomb Green Smoothie

You know I love spinach, mangoes, and berries, especially blackberries and blueberries. Not only are they loaded with pigment-based antioxidants to pump up the immune system, they also are some of the tastiest things I've ever had the pleasure of eating (or drinking). The fruit of an orange is tossed in the mix for a tangy, sweet addition to the tart/sweet berry flavors. Use baby spinach in this recipe to keep the greens tasting mild, as they should definitely take a back seat to the berries in this. Also, this is one Green Smoothie that is a must-chill, which means lots of ice chips! Here are the ingredients:

1 cup baby spinach

Fruit of 1 large orange

3/4 cup blueberries (frozen blueberries work well here if needed)

3/4 cup blackberries (frozen works here too!)

Purified water and ice chips to suit

There should be enough of this recipe for 2 servings, each containing about 130 calories, zero fat or cholesterol, 34 grams of carbohydrates, 2 grams of protein, and 3 grams of dietary fiber.

Creamy Strawberry Green Smoothie

In my family, there's no doubt that strawberries are one of our favorite food items. We all love and eat them regularly in Green Smoothie form of course. So what could be better, especially on a warm afternoon than a creamy Green Smoothie loaded with phytonutrients and tasting of tangy/sweet strawberries? These Green Smoothies are taste bud pleasers that can also help to save and elongate your life. Once again, the Green Smoothie demonstrates its ability to be a World Champion of Nutrition, while still delivering flavor and texture that would make an infant smile in contentment! Mix the following until frothy, creamy, and succulent:

1 cup mild Swiss chard

1½ cups of fresh (or frozen) strawberries

1 large banana

3/4 cup plain low-cal yogurt

2 tablespoons honey

Ice chips to suit

Note that there's no real need to add water to this recipe in most cases. The object here is creamy, not runny so if you need any water at all it won't be much! Each delicious serving offers about 200 calories, just 1 gram of fat, very low cholesterol (6 mg), a big 6 grams of protein, 4 grams of fiber, and 48 grams of carbohydrates. Enjoy them with the family!

Apple Parsley Passion Green Smoothie

You know the apple-cinnamon-crisps that so many people make right around the holidays? I know they aren't exactly health food, but I have weaknesses too, you know? I love those things and can eat way too many of them! Besides the crispy, sweet, tart delightfulness they bring to my mouth, I love the way they smell just about as much. For some odd reason (I'm really unsure why), I start thinking about those apple-cinnamon crisps every time I make this next Green Smoothie.

It contains apples and does very well with just a little pinch of cinnamon (don't overdo this). It also has cucumber and parsley in it, which makes it seem not like the crisps at all, but adds in loads of nutritious value. Here's what to use:

1 large Fuji (if possible) apple

1 cup chopped parsley

1 medium sized, peeled cucumber

1 ripe banana

1⅓ cups purified water

Ice chips to suit

It may not seem like the holidays when you drink these Green Smoothies, but it is an offering of many blessings to your body and brain. There are so many vitality-enhancing phytonutrient gifts inside that you'll swear it's Christmas!

Blissful Mango Green Smoothie

Question: What do you get when you combine sweet, juicy mangoes with a pear, a banana, and some stem less Swiss chard?

Answer: Bliss – Mango Bliss!

The Mango Bliss Green Smoothie is a true natural blessing that you should enjoy often. There are so many antioxidant phytonutrients bursting forth from each succulent serving that free radicals will be fighting each other to get out of your body! I like to go ahead and blend the Green Smoothie up, then serve it with slices of juicy kiwi. I place the kiwi on a clear saucer and serve the Green Smoothie in a frosty, clear glass. All the color and fragrances excite the senses, preparing the body for the health load to come. It's like an anti-oxidizing tank, rushing through the terrain of your body, vanquishing free radicals, and restoring your natural health levels!

2 medium mangoes

1 cup Swiss chard with stems removed

1 ripe pear

1 ripe banana

1 cup purified water

Ice chips to suit

Perfectly Delicious Green Smoothie

This next Green Smoothie recipe is totally scrumptious and is based with pears. I think d'Anjou are best (in my opinion) as they are extra sweet when properly ripe and bring an enticing texture to the blend. Also, this Green Smoothie is special because it contains aloe vera, which has been used forever as a natural health remedy, preventative substance, and treatment for various ailments and afflictions. You won't taste the aloe vera (or "feel" it) in the Green Smoothie. I recommend you experiment with aloe vera in different Green Smoothie recipes, as it adds so much to the mix without any disruption of taste and/or enjoyment. Of course, the kale and banana are both mild and super-nutritious as well. Use the following:

2 d'Anjou (if available) pears

1 cup de-stemmed kale

1 small aloe vera leaf

1 medium banana

1/2 to 3/4 cup purified water

Ice chips to suit

Frozen Carrot Ginger Zinger Green Smoothie

I feel that there's definitely something special about the combination of apples, ginger, cinnamon. and carrot. It's a classic taste that reminds me of the holidays and good family times (I never know where that comes from, but it's a good feeling). This Green Smoothie recipe delivers bunches of healing, healthful advantages, and a cool, refreshingly light taste. These are so delicious on a hot day, in the shade, served ice cold. Yummy!

I Like Swiss chard in this recipe because of the extra little zing they add. I even like chard (in this recipe anyway) better than spinach! Anyway, the ginger adds its own special blend of phytonutrients, while the apple and carrots deliver pectin, Vitamin K, fiber, and lots more. All in all, this Green Smoothie is one of the healthiest, most energizing, healing foods on the planet. Place the following ingredients in your blender and fire it up!

1 cup Swiss chard

1 large green apple

2 teaspoons freshly grated ginger root

1 cup fresh carrot juice (try freezing this first, as it's cold and delish!)

1 cup fresh-squeezed orange juice

1 tablespoon honey

1/4 teaspoon cinnamon

Ice chips to suit

Each of the 2 large servings made will deliver about 175 calories, zero fat, zero cholesterol, 41 grams of carbohydrates, 2 grams of protein, and 3 grams of fiber. You'll love the classic, light taste!

Dandy Dark Green Smoothie

You guessed right! The "Dandy" in the Dandy Dark Green Smoothie comes from dandelions. They are so loaded with unique phytonutrients and mystery that I can't help being drawn to them. Every time I tell my friends anything about dandelions, they always react with some degree of curiosity (even though they are mostly used to me sipping on unusual fruit/vegetable combos).

I'll tell you up front that this recipe is a bit on the "acquired taste" side of the Green Smoothie planet. Personally, I find them maximally delicious – but then again, I love all natural food sources. Take some time to understand the intricacies of this dark green delight and you'll be on your way to unspoiled health and longevity! Here's what to use:

1 whole bunch of dandelion greens

4 Roma tomatoes

2 to 2½ cups purified water

Ice chips to suit

Heavy Metal Detox Green Smoothie

It's definitely an international concern that we are exposed to and thereby take in, far too many heavy metals. They're in the air, ground, water, food supply, and just about everywhere else you look. Trace elements of heavy metal toxins build up in our bodies over time and we just need a little help (from Green Smoothies) to detoxify and refresh. In this recipe, cilantro, nettles. and parsley come together to give your body a cleansing blast of nutrition that it's been (literally) dying for! So when you're feeling the need to cleanse from within, blend up the following ingredients and enjoy some smooth-sippin' medicine that will make your body dance inside!

1 bunch cilantro

2 cups nettles (may require a visit to your local health food store)

1 bunch fresh parsley

2 stalks celery

Juice and pulp of 1 medium lemon

2 medium mangos

2 to 3 cups purified water

Ice chips to suit

Monster-Nute Green Smoothie

This "Monster" of a Green Smoothie is a heavyweight all the way! It combines dandelion, chard, kale, parsley, and aloe vera to create one of the healthiest concoctions in the history of the planet. Mixing these ultra-vital greens together maximizes their bio-availability and pumps your body up with disease fighting antioxidants. The pears and banana jump into the mix to add sweet tastes with extra nutrients, making this Green Smoothie a super food source that will ease ailments and fix afflictions. This recipe makes about 2 quarts of the Monster, enough to last a single person all day long. Enjoy regularly!

1/2 cup de-stemmed kale greens

1/2 cup stem less Swiss chard

1/2 bunch parsley

1 small aloe vera leaf

1/2 bunch dandelion greens

3 pears

1 banana

2 to 3 cups purified water

Ice chips to suit

Avonilla Honey Green Smoothie

Yes, I created the new word "avonilla." You see, I am a huge fan of avocados and vanilla both – and this Green Smoothie contains both – This combination blends into a super creamy, absolutely sinful taste treat for anyone who needs a super-dose of nourishment. The avocado and plain yogurt in this recipe add such rich creaminess. The pear adds sweetness and the honey adds a sophisticated note of class. All in all, the Avonilla Honey Green Smoothie is a subtle temptation that will keep you coming back to it again and again!

1 cup fresh spinach

1 medium avocado

1 pear

1/3 cup low-cal plain yogurt

1 tablespoon honey

1/3 teaspoon vanilla extract

Purified water and ice chips to suit

This recipe makes enough for 2 large servings, and each delivers just about 170 calories, only 1 gram of saturated fat, but 6 grams of unsaturated fat, a little 2 mg of cholesterol, 3 grams of protein, 3 grams of fiber, and 27 grams of carbohydrates. Delicious, creamy, refreshing, and ultimately healthful!

The Libido-Up Green Smoothie

It happens all the time: I get asked about the connections between Green Smoothies and sexual health. Although I am personally a bit skeptical about the concept of certain foods acting as powerful aphrodisiacs, I've had several of my students come back and tell me that they had some really "good" results after drinking a serving or two of The Libido-Up Green Smoothie.

You see, purslanes are naturally loaded with Vitamin C and Omega-3 fatty acids. They are succulents cultivated in more than 40 varieties. Purslanes are slightly salty and a bit sour so the flavor combines well with the limes and watermelon in this recipe. Here's what to mix:

3 cups wild purslanes

1 small watermelon

Juice and pulp from 3 limes

You probably won't need to add any water to this recipe (because of the watermelon), but ice chips are still recommended for that extra blast of cooling refreshment!

Now, as for whether it works as an aphrodisiac, you'll just have to try and judge for yourself!

Buckethead's Green Smoothie for Dogs

Buckethead is a Pit-Lab, the best dog I've ever been friends with and a serious connoisseur of Green Smoothies (dog style that is). Ol' Buckethead likes to get in on any action that may be happening, in any area, at any time he happens to be there. Of course, it follows that he likes to be a part of the Green Smoothie preparation and imbibing ceremonies at the house. Please note that Buckethead is not allowed to be a "begging bum." He is not allowed to beg food from humans. Rotten Hound! He is, however, allowed to have an occasional Green Smoothie with the Fam.

He loves them and it makes me feel really good to know that he gets to benefit from free radical destruction, increased energy, detoxification, and the rest of the Green Smoothie attributes just like the rest of his family.

Here's what to mix up for one of BH's favorite Green Smoothie recipes:

1 cup fresh kale or spinach (Buckethead approves of both)

1 large banana

1 cup purified water

2 tablespoons olive oil (BH prefers Extra Virgin!)

1 heaping teaspoon of kelp, either as a powder or in granule form

Throw in some torn-up nori sheets and let him go at it! We have also had good luck with freezing them in ice cube trays and giving Buckethead (and the rest of our pooches) frozen Green Smoothie treats here and there.

Kee-Boh's Feline Purr-fection Green Smoothie

My family also has a furry little Koo-Cat named Kee-Boh. Kee-Boh prefers to hunt, fiercely like a lion throughout the day and then returns home in the early evening, gut filled with fresh rat meat or whatever he eats out there! Of course, he has a bowl of delicious cat food at home too, but he must get most of his meals out in the fields. He is really a quite impressive hunter.

Anyway, when Kee-Boh returns to the house at night, tired and weary from the hunt, he is sometimes treated to his favorite Green Smoothie. He truly believes that his Green Smoothies are a sign of his royalty and he always gets excited like he's getting a fresh Pacific salmon or something!

Mix up Kee-Boh's favorite Green Smoothie for your kitty today with:

1 cup wheat grass (or any type of non-sprayed grass)

1 cup purified water

2 tablespoons olive oil

2 capsules fish oil (just pour the oil from the capsules over the top of   the blended smoothie)

An optional pinch of catnip (careful of the cat buzz you may induce!)

This recipe makes about 8 servings for an average cat. Like the dog-style Green Smoothies, they can be frozen in ice cube trays and served as treats. Enjoy spoiling your pets with Green Smoothies!

The Energizing Light Green Smoothie

If you're feeling low on energy, fatigued, or otherwise blah, get jacked up one of these Energizing Light Green Smoothies! I know what you're thinking: it sounds corny. But let me tell you, these smoothies will make you feel energized and light! It's true. They have just the right amount of sweet, succulent juiciness to make you feel like you're about to float away. The following recipe makes about a quart - that's 32 ounces of vitalizing love! Here's what to blend:

6 grape leaves (these have loads of resveratrol, the phytonutrient that combats aging and increases longevity)

1 cup kale

2 medium to large mangoes

1 pint fresh, ripe, organic strawberries

Seedless fruit of three oranges

No water should be needed

Ice chips to suit

You can enjoy these anytime because they are so light. Enjoy the energy boost!

Green Smoothie of Splendid Summers

The Green Smoothie of Splendid Summers is so named because it fits perfectly with hot days, cool shade, refreshing feelings, and delicate tastes. Peaches, chard, apricots, and vanilla make this Green Smoothie one of the most sophisticated and enjoyable of all. I especially like the vanilla tones it has. Mix one of these up when you've been doing yard work in the sunshine and you need to recharge and cool down. I seriously haven't met one person who tried this Green Smoothie and didn't absolutely love it.

The following recipe yields roughly 2 quarts. When the day is hot, blend the following and pour into a frosted glass. Then, sit under a shady spot and relish the day!

1 cup Swiss chard with stems removed

1 bunch fresh parsley

3 stalk celery

Fruit of 6 apricots

Fruit of 3 peaches

1/2 vanilla bean (or a dash of vanilla extract in a pinch)

1/2 to 2/3 cup purified water

Ice chips to suit

Blueberry Gold Mine Green Smoothie

Not quite sure what the name has to do with anything, but what I do know is that Blueberry Gold Mine Green Smoothies are absolutely fabulous. Mango (one of my favorites), pears, and blueberries blend so nicely with wild crafted miner's lettuce, making a smoothie that's naturally loaded with mouth-smackin' taste, powerful healing agents, and more vitamins and minerals than a health food store! The blueberries dominate this luscious concoction, bringing happiness and health to all who imbibe.

When you're in the mood for some antioxidant-filled deliciousness, mix the following in your blender until smooth:

3 cups wild crafted miner's lettuce

2 fresh, ripe pears

1/2 pint organic blueberries

About 2 cups purified water

Ice chips to suit

Mango Cocokale Green Smoothie

I pretty much love anything made with coconut. You could say I am a true coconut nut! Kale is another favorite of mine and as you may know so are mangoes. So it should be no surprise that I love this Mango Cocokale Green Smoothie! These Green Smoothie treats are exotic- tasting and refreshing, like a tropical island breeze. I take these straight to the deck in the back of the house, sit in my cozy chair, and then do some slow, smooth sipping of one of the best Green Smoothies I have ever tasted. These are tasty treats that deliver ultimate doses of holistic health!

Meat and water from a Thai coconut

1 cup fresh kale

Fruit and skin of 2 nectarines

Fruit and skin of 2 ripe peaches

Fruit and skin of 1 large mango

Purified water and ice chips to suit

The Giggling Gorilla Green Smoothie

I know. I know. Gorillas don't giggle. That's what they say, but they may not have ever had a Giggling Gorilla Green Smoothie. You see, they offer so much nutritional content and sheer deliciousness, that they may just be able to make a gorilla giggle! Although no scientific experimentation has yet been completed, I feel that there will definitely be some positive proof shown soon.

These smoothies are wonderful mixes of baby spinach, mango, banana, and orange – enough goodness to flip for! This is another Green Smoothie recipe that has a tropical taste and feel to it so, I simply have to have mine served up proper in a frosty, clear glass. With strong antioxidant content, Giggling Gorilla Green Smoothies go a long way toward making your life disease free and vibrant!

Put the following in the blender and turn on the power!

3 cups fresh baby spinach

2 medium sized ripe bananas

Fruit of 2 seedless, peeled oranges

Fruit and skin from 1 large mango

1½ to 2 cups purified water

Ice chips to suit

This recipe yields about a half gallon of Giggling Gorilla smoothness and every single drop will be most delicious indeed!

The Classic Green Smoothie

This Green Smoothie is a juicy blend of health-packed nutrients. It's an excellent representative of what a classic Green Smoothie should look, taste, and feel like (at least that's how I see it). It combines miraculously vital kale greens with Granny Smith apples, banana, and parsley to yield a deep green smoothie that excites the senses.

I made one for my husband just last week and he said that it made him feel like Superman! It's simple to make, quick to clean up after, a messenger of holistic health, and a genuinely tasty treat! Here's what to mix in the blender:

1 cup kale greens, stems removed

2 Granny Smith apples

1 large, ripe banana

1/2 cup fresh parsley leaves

2 cups water

Ice chips to suit

You may need to add a bit more water, depending on the size and moisture content of the fruits you use. Made as above, this recipe makes 2 good servings. Each serving contains just over 100 calories, no saturated fats whatsoever, no cholesterol, low sodium, 4 grams of fiber, more than 2 grams of protein, and 26 grams of carbohydrates. This is another one of those Go-To Green Smoothies and using simple ingredients is quick and easy!

Blueberry Flax Attack Green Smoothie

Ready to get attacked? I mean attacked by a blast of antioxidants and heart healthy Omega-3 fatty acids of course! This recipe for the Blueberry Flax Attack Green Smoothie will rock your world with high levels of madly beneficial phytonutrients and other goodies. It's hard to go wrong when you combine the intricate flavors of blueberry, banana, honey, and flax seeds. This Green Smoothie recipe is great for treating the symptoms associated with various health conditions and diseases including, but never limited to, cardiovascular disease, atherosclerosis, multiple cancers, stroke, arthritis, hypertension, diabetes, and more. Now, that is Big Medicine! Try these ingredients in the blender:

1 cup fresh kale greens, no stems

1 large, ripe banana

1 cup fresh or frozen blueberries

1 cup low-cal plain yogurt

4 tablespoons flax seeds

1 tablespoon organic honey

Purified water and ice chips to suit taste and texture preferences

This recipe will make enough for 2 servings, each containing about 225 calories, 2 grams of saturated fat, 2 grams of unsaturated fat, 5 grams of fiber, 8 grams of protein, very low cholesterol, and 42 grams of carbohydrates. It's hard to beat as a source for optimal nutrition. The Blueberry Flax Attack Green Smoothie has the power to make humans thrive!

King of Antioxidants Green Smoothie

Last, but not least for Green Smoothie recipe #51, I'll tell you a little story. You see, I get so many questions about the best Green Smoothie for antioxidant content. My answer is always the same, that all Green Smoothies are loaded with antioxidants. Some more than others, yes, but all Green Smoothies are super food sources – absolutely flooded with antioxidants and many other health-driving elements.

Anyway, back to the story. My husband always jokingly refers to himself as the "King" of our "castle." So for my King, I thought about the best sources of antioxidants, made them into a Green Smoothie recipe and then called it the King of Antioxidants Green Smoothie. I want him to live a long, long time and want to do what I can to help make sure that happens. So what could be more antioxidant-loaded than acai, blueberries, pomegranates, and bananas?

This monster of the antioxidant realm is fully lip-smacking and very, very healthy! It tastes so good that you'll swear you're at an expensive health spa, getting spoiled and pampered. Just take the following ingredients, put them in the blender, work with the purified water and ice, and blend it all up until it's smooth and ready. (Note the acai and pomegranate juice instead of whole fruits. This is only because in many areas, it's difficult to find fresh pomegranates and acai berries.)

2 cups kale greens (or your favorite green leafy vegetable)

1/3 cup fresh pomegranate juice

1 ounce whole acai berry juice

2 cups fresh blueberries (freeze them to add coldness to the mix!)

2 medium, ripe bananas

Purified water and ice chips to suit

Each extra delicious serving will supply your system with almost 400 calories, only 1 gram of fat, 3 grams of protein, and 102 grams of carbohydrates. This antioxidant-rich Green Smoothie is powerful, effective medicine. It can literally add years to your life if consumed regularly.

So drink up!

Conclusion

So there we are – loads of information about how and why Green Smoothies are some of the world's best food sources in terms of nutritional value, taste, and health benefits. However, what's even more impressive about Green Smoothies is that there is an entire international subculture developing in their wake. People around the planet are beginning to understand just how imperative it is to maintain optimal nutritional levels. They understand that choosing the correct foods can elongate life and make living more enjoyable along the way.

When you regularly give your body the nutrients it needs to function optimally, it will reward you back by thinking, moving, feeling, and looking better. Your body is an amazing machine that needs quality fuel to perform to its best. So please take the time to develop good Green Smoothie habits and deeply incorporate them in your life. You and your entire family will benefit in so many powerful ways.

Enjoy Green Smoothies for life!

Made in the USA
San Bernardino, CA
08 March 2014